Poetry After
PHIL VE

C000176782

SPM Publications
London

SPM Publications
www.spmpublications.com
publisher@spmpublications.com

First published in the United Kingdom by SPM Publications – an imprint
of Sentinel Writing & Publishing Company in August 2020.

ISBN 978-1-9162263-1-9

Sentinel Writing & Publishing Company is a style of SPM Publications Ltd.

Set in Garamond 9 – 16 points
Cover Art: Angelus Novus by Paul Klee (1920)
Book & Cover Design by Nnorom Azuonye

Writing poetry after Auschwitz is barbaric.
- Theodor Adorno.

Acknowledgments

My thanks to the editors of the following magazines, anthologies and websites in which some of these poems have appeared: Acumen, Anima, Crannóg, Early Works, Elbow Room, Firewords, Gold Dust, Ink Sweat and Tears, Out of Place, Pennine Platform, Salzburg Poetry Review, The Curlew, The Kent and Sussex Folio, The Poetry Shed, and The Road to Clevedon Pier.

'Interpreting', 'Wedding day' and 'Deceit' previously appeared in a Stickleback micro-collection *This Quieter Shore*, published by Hedgehog Poetry Press.

Several poems were runners-up or shortlisted in competitions: 'Flax' in the Ealing Festival Competition in 2015; '1955' in the Binsted Festival Poetry Competition in 2016; 'The wall' and 'The dried flower arranger' in the Shepton Mallet Snowdrop Festival Poetry Competition in 2017; and 'Buzzard' in the Fosseway Competition 2017. 'El Tres de Mayo' won the Kent and Sussex Poetry Society's Keith Francis prize in 2016 and the Zealous.co poetry prize in 2018; the title poem 'Poetry after Auschwitz' also won the Keith Francis Prize, in 2019.

Thanks are due to various members of the Kent and Sussex Poetry Society and Nicholas Bielby for their generous editorial advice on several poems.

The epigram from Theodor Adorno is from *Prisms*. Translated from the German by Samuel and Shierry Weber. MIT Press, 1997.

The quotation on page 49 is from Walter Benjamin's *Theses on the Philosophy of History, IX*, collected in Illuminations (Translated by Harry Zohn), Schocken Books, New York, 1969.

The quotation on page 35 is from *One Robe, One Bowl, The Zen Poetry of Ryōkan,* translated by John Stevens. Weatherhill, Boston, 1997.

Contents

Poetry After Auschwitz

This book is dedicated with love to my parents
Anne and David Vernon

Poetry after Auschwitz

'Poetry is pointless – like kicking a stone'
- overheard at a poetry reading

At the start and the end of this long, straight road:
a silent child, a house in flames,
a leafless tree, an empty town

He kicks a stone to watch it leap
and skitter on the flattened clay,
then slow and stall and go to ground

Along the forest edge stand those
he's failed to save, he sings his song;
his unknown patrons hear no sound

and yet he feels their silence deep
beneath his feet, and sees beyond
the tree, the child, the house, the town

El Tres de Mayo

The edge of town. A lantern lights the man
about to die. His comrades clasp their eyes.
He kneels: arms spread like sails aloft, he wills
defiance but it's terror which obtains.

The friar murmurs blessings, swears and damns
the French. The waiting chorus moans and cries,
then 'tirez!', muskets fusillade; he spills
beside the corpses slumped among the stains.

Low fearful wails behind the victims' hands,
the panicked mumbling of the priest who shrives
the doomed, the terse command, the gunshots – still
they resonate, among the faint remains

of ancient susurrus of surf on sand,
dead families' and lovers' truths and lies,
muezzin, birdsong, rain on roof tiles, peals
of laughter, angelus and lonesome trains.

Each wave, since noise and atmosphere began,
continuously pales but never dies:
each instant as it passes, pares and steals
a half, and then a half, and half again...

reducing history from the first big bang
towards a point it will not realise:
attenuated, yet its core prevails,
diminishing, but nowhere vanishing.

What's past is present: faded cryptogram
of sound – no matter if we try to prise
a meaning out of or ignore it – fills
our ears with its abiding, quiet refrain:

the edge of town. A lantern lights the man
about to die. His comrades clasp their eyes.
He kneels, arms spread like sails aloft, he wills
defiance but it's terror which obtains.

The nurseryman

and then the government attacked
and fire leapt from roof to roof
and all the colours bled to black
for days the greatest rainstorm sluiced
the soot from stumps of home to stain
the soil I lost my wife to war
our girl to floods our boy to flames
I fled with only what I wore
I hid in fields in ditches – nights
I named the rose I bred for each
repeatedly and hugged them tight
I walked in circles weeks then reached
this pebbled shore at Dungeness
awaiting boats to France or death

Ḥērem

And they utterly destroyed all that was in the city,
both man and woman, young and old, and ox, and sheep,
and ass, with the edge of the sword. Joshua 6:21

and when we heard the trumpets sound
our orders were to swarm amid
the people of the place and end
them as they fled or stood or hid

or rose half dead from underground

compel those few souls who still lived
to haul their children women men
and build a burning pyramid
beyond the flattened walls and town
it was our fate and charge to rid
of every human soul we found

in faith we did as we were bid

Ḥērem: the total destruction of the enemy and their goods.

12

The bridge

I come each day to clean the marble plaque,
place flowers beneath Arzadin's face, and pray
he rests in peace. The eve of the attack,
he begged my blessing which I proudly gave –
a mother's leave to die.
                    Low sunlight bathes
the bridge, the road, the bracken-covered hills
in warmth and welcome; piebald peaks arrayed
against the sky stand friendly guard.
                            War steals
our children but it spares them all the ills
of longer life, and us from saving them.
I sit in simple silence simply filled
with comfort by his being near.
                        She spends
her evenings at the bridge contentedly;
the sunlight dissolves gently in the sea.

Shiva

Rice crowded terraced heights above
in vivid stripes
as though the world had not
for a long moment paused
while a harsh and violent wind seared the slopes,
and the city they'd for years
led down towards
had not
in that long moment gone

though when you drop a bomb
however powerful
some features randomly remain intact
or recognisable, at least

a chimney stack
a temple arch, a river course, a grid
of curiously uncluttered streets
a simple shed
a jagged obelisk of stones –
the relic corner of a vanished home
in a vanished neighbourhood

I heard you say
your sister's blood would not stop flowing in
the hot summer sun;
she could not swallow
to replace the blood she lost, she was
a child – and so
were you –

it feels like yesterday.

To say goodbye

I walked

through unmown grass
and tumbled graves

We talked
a little

spoke of irony
(you smiled
I thought)

And then
next day
unknown to me

you died

The pallbearer

The bell falls quiet; the horses' shoes collide
with cobbles; music floats; the priest appears.
We measure off our height in equal pairs,
absorb the coffin's weight and, eyes downcast,
in tentative half-march, proceed inside.

June's brightness filters limpid through stained glass
into a cool obscurity. Song climbs
from choir to fill the space, and all combines
in Dean Donne's Equal Music, Equal Light,
to ease us, leaving but two questions at the last.

What makes a well-lived life good, in our sight?
The mourners praise her as a wife, her art,
the way she raised her children, her kind heart.
Was that enough, how do we set the bar?
Had she done more, might they still more delight?

And what is left of us, when what we are
dissolves? A pigeon perches in the beams
and causes quite a stir, her soul it seems,
ascending – mumbo jumbo, surely: wings
as apt to rouse, as raise her to a star.

The vicar sprinkles holy water, sings
the final phrases as his curate swings
the censer, then we shoulder her again.
I'd swear she's lighter now than when we came –
not by the weight of her departed flame –
but since to pray together strengthens us within.

Loss

I met you only briefly, twice,
perhaps a dozen years ago
beneath the pinnacles of ice
you feared. I wonder, often: did you sow
those seeds you held, into the melted snow?

You stood there slight, but this stood out:
you were a powerhouse of grief;
alone. And certain – way past doubt –
of utter undeception, in whose teeth
you'd lost your grip of comfortable belief.

So deep, so deep, you felt distress,
it stayed unburied, near to hand,
from where you vouched your forthright sense
the gods, with arbitrary spite, had planned
to visit drought upon and scorch your land.

I screwed my eyes against the glare
of highland light which bathed, and drained
all life, from the deserted square;
I wanted nothing, nothing more, right then
than for you to be healed and whole again,

and still, today, I think of you
abandoned – brittle, proud – by grace.
I pray you found a pathway through
the melting snow to reach a burial place
wherein to plant anew; a safer space.

The scent of green

I've all I need: my books, TV, a view
of sparrows and squirrels in the apple tree;
and when they mow the lawn, I almost dare
breathe unlost summers in the scent of green.

Other girls never returned to their life before –
I quietly hid my uniform, away
from where my hands might search the wardrobe rail,
and placed my demob bag in the attic, to fade.

My family welcomed me to their routines,
but the clouds of peace hung heavy on our home
and no-one wanted more for me, nor seemed
to wish me to want more, than I'd once known.

I couldn't wish what they did not, nor keep
my raw imagination under rein:
she flew too fast – and when horizons loomed
she shied, I fell; and never rode again

and half forgot I'd shared a bond, dark hours
and dreams with friends, and helped to win a war,
and danced the conga in Trafalgar Square.
Days pass. In here I'm safe; I'm fed; I'm warm.

Glimpse

Throughout your life, you suffered prejudice:
a look, a word, the absence of a word,
led you to add offenders to your list –
though what they'd said was seldom what you'd heard.

And yet to those who knew their place, and yours,
as I did naturally, you shone so bright
we basked, and took for granted the applause
accorded – sought by – you, was yours by right.

When your candescence died before you did,
if you knew us, or you, you gave no sign;
we prayed you weren't aware of how you lived –
the helplessness, the odour of decline,

your not quite puzzled commentary and tone:
'I knew you yesterday; don't make that face;
my brother's ship is due; is this my home?'
And then withdrawal: an empty pupa case.

One morning like today, in spring's chaste light
you drew me close – you knew me after all –
and whispered 'I went to the edge last night –
they held me back – they should have let me fall'.

In that clear glimpse before the clouds closed in
again, your hopeless eyes told me you knew.
We kept your flame alight but faltering.
And now, I struggle to remember you.

The funeral

We came from far, and others too, to say
farewell. Amidst the stony faces and the tears,
a feud was healed. The southern sun shone. Prayers
were said and sung. Things did go wrong: the grave
knee-deep in mud, the priest who disappeared,
the Mass delayed, the coffin stuck – one half
inside, one out; her name and epitaph
misspelled – flawed both in life and death. She'd steered
unschooled, with strength and fear, past flotsam thrown
about by giant seas of change. She'd clung
to some, eyes closed. She'd been both helped and hurt.
She'd helped and hurt – and led. We closed the stone
lid, spoke of special moments, good she'd done;
more quietly of things which had not worked.

Letting down

There are péchés véniels of letting down:
the dates and deadlines missed, the cards unsent,
implied commitments quietly disavowed,
and un-run errands; small forgettings. Then
the more important kind: the two men dead
because of things he failed to do; the pains
ignored, solicitations left unsaid:
his ceaseless failure to untangle shame
from guilt. You swam in swelling waters and
I looked away. You wandered unprepared
into the badlands; I could only stand
there as your voice grew ever fainter – scared
to act. You're still not safe. I still can't move.
I let down furthest, those I'm closest to.

My weather girl

Tonight you told us our tomorrow will
    be changeable, though starting dry.
You spoke with all the confidence instilled
    by science and facts – but I could see
anxiety alive behind your eyes.

They spoke of unslept nights, of the debris
    and disarray of home where dawn
no longer gracefully unfolds, but bleeds
    a crimson warning to the day;
of weather fronts where storm clouds follow storm.

The data show that winter's here to stay,
    but you persist with your forecast
of early spring, where daffodils display
    above the snow, proof of the heat
still stored below. It will not come to pass:

your husband's love affair with self-defeat
    ensures that every sign of thaw,
however mild, is just one more deceit
    before the sky turns dark again
and elements resume their climate war.

His voice, as you drive home in sheets of rain,
    reveals he's turned once more to face
the buffets of the private hurricane
    he mocks and dares to do its worst –
from his retreat within the sham embrace

of grape or grain. You close your phone and curse.
    Your stomach seeps with acid fear,
uncertain if the threatening clouds will burst
    upon the night ahead. I share
your dread, and drink my numbness deep and fast,
    to be inert when you reach here.

Reservoir

Your eyelids flicker while you sleep
in filtered moonlight, and betray
a reservoir of dark, hid deep,
swept ceaselessly by squalls which play
and whip the waves, until sunrise
when you assume a veil to view
yourself and those around you through
and shroud your secrets from your eyes.

He offered love without entail
while hers was rationed, rare, withdrawn:
they wove cold, angry, constant, warm
and doubting colours in your veil,
distorting what you see and feel,
and storing hurt, too deep to heal.

Twenty-five years
For Tebo

I waken too early, on woodsman's toes explore
a home that's still, until our neighbour turns
the news up loud, and you begin to snore
to match the rhythm of the morning trains.

Again I discover as though surprised, the sounds
of dawn are sung by modern life not birds,
that we inhabit cul-de-sacs, not glades,
wear dressing gowns, not bark cloth capes or furs.

So coffee and toast, and a view of the low winter sky,
an hour or two at tasks brought home from work:
I read, respond, review, redraft, delay,
and listen out for when I hear you stir.

We make pastel love, and when we look outside
a quiet snow has fallen across the town.
The sun shines on the whitened roofs and road.
We smile and put the central heating on.

Interpreting

We had little to do at first
except avoiding one another's eye
with manufactured hurt –
as one of the Russians (quietly) remarked:
translating stony silences
is harder than you'd think.

When Khrushchev demanded Ike apologise
for what was practically an act of war
Ike made like nothing had been said –
though we'd all heard it had,
and I'd repeated it
so I was sure.

But Khrushchev wouldn't let it go:
it was yet more proof he couldn't trust the West,
so what was the point of this?
Then Ike said we'd had no choice
because we can't trust you –

and so the summit went:
an injured silence interspersed with versions of
it's all your fault,
until the Soviets said that's that and quit the room
and Paris, too.

I heard all both sides said out loud –
said half of it myself, in fact –
but cannot say if either asked himself
how his opponent felt, nor how
to help him help make this all right.

Wedding day

Look at us then: my buttonhole, your pearls,
your hand in mine, our smiles with energy
enough to make the harbour flags unfurl –
and as we placed our hands upon the wheel
we chose our course, and when to put to sea.

Our wedding gifts were lost in violence.
The boat flung us like flotsam as she heeled
and plunged. With reckless seamanship – with senseless
will – with ragged sails – we pitched our way
and frightened crew through torment and ordeal.

Look at us now: our boat survived the storms,
scraped past the reef and, limping to this bay
fetched us together on this quieter shore –
our weathered hands guiding the wheel no more,
but touching one another when they may.

Im Abendrot

For Mona and Paksie

O weiter, stiller Friede!
So tief im Abendrot.
Wie sind wir wandermüde...
    - Joseph von Eichendorff

I've stood, transfixed, as perfect darkness hangs
its velvet for a million fireflies' perfect glow,
heard silence sliced in two as choirs sang,
awoken on the moor to silent snow;

breathed in the distant scent of desert rain,
felt sun desert the deep ravine like ebbing tide
as eagles called from tree to tree, and seen
a future in your future mother's eyes.

Now voice and strings stretch taut and fall away
through open windows to the night: and steal
my chance to share those times with you when skies

blew clear, small sounds sailed far, and joy and pain
held one another still. And you will feel
your sun retreat and know your own fireflies.

Solidarity

My fathers fouled your fathers' wells,
unpicked the fabric of their land,

retuned the air with chapel bells,
condemned their crops as contraband,

abased each woman, shamed each man,
renamed their children as despair.

And so the years of waste began:
my fathers' legacy laid bare.

Am I – their child – allowed to care
for mine – their victims' heirs – today?

Am I allowed to empathise
as they contend with disrepair?

Is there a penance I can pay
so I can know my children's lives?

The fat and the lean

When spending patterns oscillate
between low river flow and spate,
while income falls like intermittent rain,
and you must save or borrow, or
survive without till you can pay –
remember, as you ford
a streambed turned to dust
or hold your head above the flood,
that money's never worth so much
as when it serves as metaphor
for love.

Chiaroscuro
Finding the 14th Dalai Lama

Standing as if to one side,
I saw us blow through raw chapped hands
to rouse the dying fire
and busy ourselves preparing tea,

in small talk and in minor tasks,
to hide our frightened desire,
exchanging a rapid, freighted glance
then looking away

at the horses hobbled half in shade,
dark sacks, stitched roughly closed and rimed with frost,
the children stirring drifts
of sunlit smoke and dust
cut through by morning shadows –

anything, not
to allow ourselves to watch
the boy who, motionless –
almost amused – watched us,
then reached
to claim the hidden rosary,
unerringly.

Later,
squatting beside the barley sacks,
he nodded and touched each artefact
his Holiness had owned and –
almost amused –
rejected the rest,
unerringly.

A man of faith – a poet –
I'm intimate with doubt
and can't decide if we picked him, he us,
or – if it's destiny, then whose?

But I shed my unbelief as he —
almost amused —
picks out a path through shade and light,
unerringly.

What we are afraid to tell our children

Before you start, best think it through;
more hands, light work; more haste, less speed;
take care, in all the things you do,
of others' feelings, others' needs:
treat them as you'd have them treat you.

All these and other rules of thumb,
words of advice and basic truth,
elders have garnered one by one,
and willingly pass on – as proof
against disquiet – to the young.

But out of fear, there's one they won't:
that arguments for quitting life
are barely weaker, more remote –
once you weigh happiness and strife –
than reasons why we mostly don't.

The sop

And when He had dipped the sop,
He gave it to Judas Iscariot, the son of Simon.
Then said Jesus unto him,
That thou doest, do quickly. - John, 14: 26-27.

You liked to walk alone in the warm dark wind
and slow your heart to beat in measured time.
'Come too', you said that night. 'We'll take the wine.
I'd like your views on how the movement's grown,
and what the coming days will bring.'

We passed the dogs and left the homes
and murmured dialogues behind; and paced
the quiet lanes where branches interlaced
but failed to shield us from the frailty
and ache, and weight, of night's vast dome.

'It's only you I trust, to help me free
them from the steady drip of alkali
which calcifies compassion in a lie,'
you said, 'because, alone among them all,
your love of truth exceeds your love for me.'

I felt the breeze abruptly fall,
and then your fingertips upon my hand
as, with taut tenderness, you shared your plan
to leave us violently; what I would do.
Above us in the trees, an owl called.

The day we met, my soul was damned.
The thing you tasked me with, I carried through.
At once, I fell; leaves fell; night fell; I'm lost,
with no horizons nor relief. Because
my love of truth exceeds my love for you?

Lincoln

I read the story of your death and cried
as though I'd heard the news of it, my love
not lessened by the century that divides
my time from yours; your limpid prose enough
to open to me how you layered the stuff
of tragedy within your soul – and then
absorbed again, again, again the nation's grief,
and raised yourself to rouse and rally them.

You piloted the raft in its descent
and calmed and shaped the currents till they bore
you to the ocean; touched your people's fears;
gave them the words to utter their intent.
Yet your scarred self ordained you could no more
return their love, than mine across these years.

Ryōkan

'I long to walk with another who has left the world far behind –
but no-one comes.'

Oh Ryōkan! I too long to walk with you.
You've left the world far too completely for that.

But you left behind signs: a man
can know Truth and God, yet

not lose his love of, nor surprise at
nature's small things – drunken

farmers' conversation; the
delicate yellow and blue of spring flowers.

I dreamed, long ago, of an old age like yours:
a return to the world before taking last leave –

and tried, through sitting and right-reading,
to set foot on The Path. Alas,

I still confuse rivers with mountains, and
regret spent time. But

through your words I know and love you –
and the salt of your wise, held-back tears.

Eyes
For Goya

You painted duchesses and kings as who
they were – not whom they wished to be – and gave
them what they wanted nonetheless. You drew
the inner contours of their souls; engraved
in permanence their fleeting light and shade
to share a tincture of humanity
with who would see. With care you weighed and made
each mark in a seditious tracery
of progress. Chronicler and refugee
of war, your inner turmoil matched your times:
from deep within your silence you perceived
and stilled the moment, and with tints and lines
you offer us a glimpse through people's eyes
of history as its brushstroke touched their lives.

Deceit

What if in fact Potemkin built real towns,
but sailed his empress Catherine instead
past those facades for which he's more renowned,
erected proud along the river's edge,

and wooed her thus not as befits a queen
but any girl he wanted to impress
with picnics where the Dnieper laps pristine
flood meadows with intent and tenderness,

and beached their boat beneath cascading willows,
served her champagne, caviar and dates,
and lay, caressed by wavelets in the shallows
with her, far removed from cares of state?

For any mighty fool can relocate
a bunch of scurvy settlers from the east –
it takes a rarer talent to create
the perfect backdrop for a royal tryst.

The beauty of Potemkin villages
is you can visit when – with whom – you wish,
and no one's lurking in the shadows as
a prince and empress steal a real kiss.

The small things goddesses do

In ancient Greece, a goddess, nymph
or god was always near at, and
prepared to lend a helping hand
to make a herdsman from a prince,
a shipwrecked sailor reach the shore,
and war from peace, or peace from war.
Too neat, I always thought, too neat...

Until, collapsed from drink and stress
in a London park, and hauled to my feet
and then let fall, by CID,
an Aphrodite in a summer dress
appeared, with the warmest smile,
and sat with me as I revived
enough to shuffle, sheepish, home,
while she returned to the hills, alone...

And when they set the pumps to flood
the Athens park, beneath whose shrubs
we'd slept, and sent us scurrying with
our sleeping bags for higher ground,
Demeter, dressed in widow's black,
emerged unbid from dawn to give
us carrier bags of bread and grapes,
then turn and walk away
without a further glance or sound.

So they were right, the poets, that
the gods descend in mortal shape
and influence the course we take:
slight variances of fate, perhaps –
no major shifts of plot; as acts
of kindness surely cannot not
impact how those they touch proceed,
nor how they impact those they touch
in turn...

But are they kindnesses?
We count as playthings merely, seen
from Mount Olympus, and I need
to ask those careless goddesses
who squandered intercession on
my undeserving youth, have I
exhausted all my share?

There's neither shade nor sky. I watch
you slump against the hollow rim
of where what's yet to come, or gone,
is dried and lifted by the wind
to fall and fleck the dunes; you dare
not dream nor raise your eyes beyond
horizons where the haze begins.

I do, and see that neither what
nor how we pray, makes any odds
at all to goddesses who change
the views they look down on, at whim,
between this arid lowland, and
a valley blessed by quiet rain.

The visitors' book at the Knoydart bothy

"Three hundred miles by train and bus,
fifteen on foot, just to spend a night
with the woman I love. Has it come to this?"
I read in muted peat firelight.

I pictured him: a wife, two kids,
a month of scheming, then to crest
a ridge and share a gasp amidst
this vast, receding endlessness;

a mutual glance, his arm around
her shoulder, hers about his waist;
their futures and dilemmas drowned
by silence, resonance and space.

And his exquisite moment pierced
my carapace, exquisitely.
The peat smoke lifted acrid fears
across the room, and clung to me

thereafter, placing next ahead
of now: glimpsed oceans, distant peaks
still beckoned but dispersed – the red
armada, drifting out of reach.

And so I traded wilderness
for suburbs where, late nights, I draw
peat smoke, uncanny loneliness
and mountains: shadows on the wall.

My next self-portrait

At dusk in a beach-front window, where
the welcome shadows of half-light
obscure his still and empty hands –
the glass of wine just out of sight;

in a comfortable chair, but ill at ease,
positioned awkwardly askew;
his face set hard, unwarmed by smile
or charm – withdrawn from public view:

my sitter eyes the passing world
as from afar, a kind of show
which, as I sketch him, he portrays
in patterns of his own, and so

protects himself from what he's done.
Redeeming features? Few, but one
stands out: examine how he scans

the waves with anxious fear, and though
he tries, can't hide that he can't know
how the ebbing tide will shape the sands.

Catherine writes home from the Via Appia

After the Romans subdued the insurrection led by Spartacus,
they crucified more than 6000 slaves along 130 miles of the Via Appia.
*   – Nineteenth century guide book.*

A cold, dry wind blows hollow through the hearts
of travellers from Capua to Rome;
a cross set every thirty paces marks
their haunted progress northward and reminds
them uniformly, order outweighs stone.

Uncountable, the undrawn souls consigned
to void, unnamed in epitaph or song...
Conflict is human history's constant bride;
her dowry underwrites a wedding feast
for which both invitation list and night are long.

With fewer wars today, by learning peace
we darkly learn ourselves: is it enough
we see the cruelty in war decrease
and yet sustain it, plainly hidden among
the dancing shadows of our winter hearth?

All hurt is felt and meted out by one
and every violence is intimate:
upon each cross a soldier nails a man.
Each night I shrink and tighten, and await
the terror of your voice, your breath, your hand.

1955

Magpies love a rabbit halfway dead –
to peck its weeping eyes, disdain the rest
then nonchalantly pause and lift their heads,
hop down and pick their way along the vale
of pain to blind and leave undead, the next.

Romans loved rabbits, too: their settlers sailed
with does and bucks, as well as laws and peace.
We love them less – we've placed them on a trail
where gun-green birds glint in the April sun,
imperious at their casual charnel feast.

We met the halfway dead, half hidden among
the dead, as we advanced towards Berlin.

I lift the stricken rabbits one by one,
take cover from their blank and aimless stare,
then break their necks and set them down within
the shadowed margins of the coppice, where
last autumn's leaves lie cold and half decayed.

The magpies scatter but they reappear.

I'm tired of asking if this horror show
would have me save or kill, or kill to save,
and – as I watch myself deal every blow –
if Romans' clearer view of dying made
them kinder. Perhaps the feasting magpies know.

i.m. Richard Langridge, who helped liberate Belsen concentration camp. The rabbit disease Myxomatosis was introduced to Britain on his farm, in 1953. Two years later, he shot himself, by which time the number of rabbits in the country had declined by 95%.

Another country

Forever travelling on this road
between the airport and hotel

through endless flatlands, shacks and rows
of unlit, half-built concrete shells

and wind-blown shadows, he's capsized
by waves of sudden tears, that swell

with unspent memories, and tides
of hollow hurt, not quite withheld.

Car headlamps swoop on tatters blown
like prayers and caught on leafless thorns –

he knows – though knows he cannot know –
something was lost, great wrong was done

here; tastes the hollowness to come,
and cries because he cannot mourn.

Freedom zone

She pauses, lowers the blinds,
departs, the taxi pulls away,
she starts to leave herself behind;

sheds what her check-in baggage weighs,
the life her passport photo knows,
and layer by layer, herself decays,

dissolves… and then a new self grows,
holds court in the airport bar, portraying
an image drawn from movie roles.

The boarding pass still bears her name,
but unmoored, in the here and now
of transit, she can choose the game

and players, set the rules for how
they'll play, and use her new-found flair
for risk to seize the winner's crown.

The tannoy sounds. In striplight glare
the five-card poker hands she deals
are the columns and rows of solitaire.

Later she picks at her in-flight meal,
sobs silently at the film that's shown,
at what the dark almost reveals:

to travel in this neither zone
simply unshackles her to feel
yet more detached, yet more alone.

Foreign correspondent

The uplands deadened him the more:
where people neatly laid in rows
called louder than in other wars,
by simple geometry; he closed

his ears but year on year the song
joined whispers from elsewhere, to drown
the voice insisting we prolong
our lives. He hears no music now.

Daybreak unrolls – without a sound
the empty landscape is unmasked,
the wind has dropped; and far from sea,

the gulls fly, quiet, above the town.
How wide, the space between what passed
and what he told of tragedy.

The girl in the swimming pool

It's magical to watch a girl begin to drown,
suspended with her face towards the rain,
then lift and place her gently on the ground
and coax her lungs to believe and breathe again.

Your dad had raced the tide, and fought his way
through surf, on jagged granite, years before,
to reach and rescue you from panicked spray
and the pull of the sea, and swim you back to shore.

You fancy higher powers had bid him save
you, so you'd later rescue in her turn
this girl half-floating on her enchanting wave
who sank, and rose, and sank; a stricken bird –

but when you lean out from the parapet
above the shadowed gorge, where far below
those blue and sightless swollen dolls forget,
forget, forget, in time with the river, you know

one life saved means no more nor less, beside
whole families who cowered in stands of cane
and, hopeless, queued in quiet lines to die,
than one life saved: unlinked in any chain.

Dictator

You take me to task because a man has died.
I ask: do you think I can just forget?
Know this: to protect what's left to protect
I won't stop short of murder when required.

We won't return to unreaped harvests, heads
bent over crippled stalks; the awkward shapes
in stiff repose; the thrice-abandoned space
bereft of you, the slaughterers, the dead.

Democracy will wait until I fear
no more the clattered landing of the crow
in silent farmland, nor that salt-sweet smell.

In quiet moments now, the sounds I hear
are not the cries of twenty years ago –
but their foretokened echoes, should I fail.

Debris

Svetlana Alliluyeva remembers her father, Josef Stalin,
in the time after her mother Nadhezda's suicide

After the comma of that night
you stood remote, continuing
to feed the angel's appetite:
in radiating circles, you
made offerings of whom you might.

In violent winds you heaped us all,
rain-soaked, debris upon debris –
a votary with trains of corn.
But no tribute would be enough
to still your angel, nor the storm

that filled and stretched his giant wings:
gales fuelled by timeless agony
and unheard cries, propelling him
towards what neither he nor time
could see, no more than could the wind;

nor still the second angel, who,
unsated, hurtled forward, blind
to where he'd travelled from, or through,
eyes only on the end. And for
them both, their stoutest servant: you.

[The Angel of History's] face is turned toward the past. Where we perceive a chain of events, he sees one single catastrophe which keeps piling wreckage upon wreckage and hurls it in front of his feet. The angel would like to stay, awaken the dead, and make whole what has been smashed. But a storm is blowing from Paradise; it has got caught in his wings with such violence, the angel can no longer close them.
The storm irresistibly propels him into the future to which his back his turned,
while the pile of debris before him grows skyward. The storm is what we call progress.

   - Walter Benjamin

La mise en valeur

We built a capital
in wilderness: a rude and concrete space
of buildings, edicts, votes; a practical
and systematic set of tools,
each in its given place.

You built a capital...

Some land, we paled and ploughed
and treed, transforming scenes we didn't know,
where rain and soil and temperature allowed –
near as we could – to sights and sounds
and cadences of home.

Some land, you paled and ploughed...

The more extensive wastes,
we ran our beasts among – patrolling lines
we'd drawn, and writing legends of the days
heroic, dust-blown riders raced
to one another's side.

The more extensive wastes...

We wielded books of law
to tame the sullen, conquered people who
defied the passage of the conqueror
resolved to cow or tame the raw
terrain – and tame him too.

You wielded books of law...

From deep beneath the earth
we lifted rust-brown rock, converting it
to prizes of far greater sheen and worth
by wit of man, than left as dirt
undug, untouched, unlit.

50

From deep beneath the earth…

Within our new domain,
new ways of seeing emerged: romantic songs
and images of stoic fathers, framed
by red and arid wilds, declaimed,
depicted, by their sons.

Your new domain…

Our battles won, we reached
out to the vanquished, offered them a chance
to learn our ways and in return to teach
us theirs; in this rich land a niche
where they might play their parts.

Your battles won, you reached

out… Yeah, we know all that.
I have a simpler way
to tell it. Rape. You raped
my mum, my gran, my dad,
my sister, me. All day
each day, with casual hate
you threw us to the ground,
beat us to sobbing silence, prised
us open one by one
and drilled us, looking down
with blank-faced undesire
then backed away, aslime with sweat and come.

With foresight you'd supplied
us whisky. I can vouch,
for all it burns my throat,
it hasn't let me cry
yet, nor those dull paws scratch
away the null; and won't.
You did what you did.
You fucked my arse. You showed

51

me not to hope, to see
the dawn as nightfall; with
your careless shrug to know
how little thought you gave to my defeat.

You took our kids from us,
and us from them, to teach
them they should neither want
to be like you nor us,
and us to no more wish
to form their future than
bring back the past we'd lost.
Stick figures, we live on
the edges of your story,
symbols of your past,
the empty space you found,
and of the guilt which undermines your glory.

Today I only want
to talk of land. And words.
You like to do things to
the land – you dig and plant
it, fence it, graze your herds
on it, sink shafts into
its depths, append your name
to tracts of it and trade
them, criss-cross it with towns
and roads – attempt to tame
it. Clever stuff, you've made
the land do more, be more, than we knew how.

Our words are not the same.
We walk, work, play, sleep, screw,
we hunt and garner, with
the earth. Each day is framed
by her horizons, though
we see beyond the ridge,
and journey there. And on
again. We name her parts

for how they stand, and where
they lie about the land.
She cradles us in crooked arms.
We knew ourselves by what we knew of her.

We witnessed your arrival, knew your brute
invasion, watched from wary margins while
you laid the layers on which you built
your nation. Though the sediments of hurt
and fear may one day leach away, a tide
of tears cannot dissolve our shame, your guilt.

Mysterious garden

That loosestrife overwhelms the rose
in June, which branches bow when wet,
a secret silence when it snows,
how birds change key before sunset,

that leaves now green were apple red,
where wrens build nests behind the fern,
which clematis wear velvet threads
and which wear silk: all this we've learned.

And yet, it's only as we turn
the soil, and sow and thin and hoe,
and tie the taller stems to stays,

and coax the unforeseen, and prune
to let light in, we start to know
what this year's garden wants to say.

The dried flower arranger

Dusk almost hid behind her eyes
   as with a voice of quiet tears
she handed me the columbines
   her sister's unforgiving man
had picked, the day he reappeared,
   still labelled in his brutal hand:
Our love is stronger than your lies.

They bring me flowers to preserve,
   my clients: quiet memorials
to love, death, marriage, birth;
   to people, moments, days now past –
parched, pastel talismans that pull
   like tides upon the heart and cast
their fragile shadows on the earth.

I work in silence. When the shop
   bell rings I read the blooms and how
they're brought – a bridal bouquet dropped
   with nonchalance, a frail fern leaf
less held than touched, the tightly-wound
   ivy and easter lily wreath,
a chaos of forget-me-nots…

I give them what they come here for:
   a clue to whom they may have been;
a bar to whom they might become.
   I can't preserve, much less restore
that April day, nor all those dreams
   we shared under the springtime sun.
I've kept the primroses I wore.

The wall

Long peace with France had softened us,
but life at home was never still.
God knows we fought, often enough,
and hard, about money, the mill,
your family – everything – until

we wore each other down, and learned
the art of never being where
the other was; and in return
somehow negotiated air
enough to breathe; and layer by layer

we built a wall: on your side home,
the church, community; you made
our children yours and yours alone.
On mine, the town, the milling trade,
the rarest snowdrops ever grown.

No other thrill can match the lurch
of coiled desire I felt each year
as new-bred snowdrop stems appeared,
and promised petals – unshed tears –
in unseen whites and greens emerged;

nor disappointment match my hurt,
that winter every snowdrop failed
to bloom, dissolving in the dirt,
and loosing suddenly a gale
of silence louder than I'd heard.

And then, as though you'd waited long
for this, you stepped across the wall
and stilled my silence, broke my fall,
and gave a plantsman lessons on
the way to shelter plants from storms.

James Allen (1832-1906) – the 'Snowdrop King' –
A miller and amateur plantsman, grew over 100
snowdrop varieties in Shepton Mallet, Somerset. But after
decades of intensive breeding, his collection was all but
wiped out by fungal and insect infestations.

The widower

The mourners gone, he felt no need
to mark her passing with a stone:
her ashes swirled into the wind
to fly or fall where they'd be blown,

as fields and copses called her name
in silence louder than he'd known,
on hillsides permanently changed,
and paths he'd now patrol alone.

He stripped the house on to the lawn –
wallpaper, sofa, tables, phones,
chairs, carpets, clothes – and burned it all:
a perfect pyre of what they'd owned...

and turned his back upon the flames
to pick a single rose she'd grown,
then sat and watched its slow decay
for days, within their hollow home.

Budding

Each time you choose a rootstock, and
the apple type to grow,

each time you excise bud from shoot,
and trim its trailing heel,

each time you slice and lift the bark,
and tease apart the 'T'

to slide and splice, and twist the tape,
and seal the scion home —

where tissue touches tissue it
already seems to know —

the knife you hold's been held and shaped
and grazed on oil and stone,

by hands that grew and planted all
the orchards you can see,

but every cut you make's
the first, and yours, alone.

Paying respects
For Maurice

The quince you so admired each year
has blossomed – a flamenco show.
Your wallflowers have now appeared,
a golden frieze you will not know.

Your clock chimes through the party wall;
no other human sound disturbs
the creaks and phantom footfalls, nor
your silence, nor the garden birds.

You hated dark, and welcomed spring –
the chance to slough off solitude,
absorb the warmth of friends and sun.

I pray, by taking pleasure in
these sights and sounds that lifted you,
we know today as you'd have done.

Ragged lawn

'Tis an unweeded garden
That grows to seed, things rank and gross in nature
Possess it merely.
   - Hamlet act 1 sc. 2

A man came in, from time to time,
to mow and weed and hoe and trim
the ordered world you left behind.

He worked with diligence and speed,
but it was only work to him,
and then he stopped – I don't know why.

And now, my cat stalks wrens among
your ragged grass and giant weeds,
and straggling dogwood overhung

with thorns – she holds her hunter's pose
amidst damp shade and rotting leaves
where phlox once bloomed in open sun.

The perfect geometry which framed
your realm has all but decomposed –
its squares and pentagrams decayed:

this wilding hunter's paradise
where any seed or rootlet grows
is fine for birds and butterflies,
but not the garden that you made.

Winter gardens

You see your gardens in the space between
the plants, raze every weed without a trace
lest it disturb the balance of your scheme,

deadhead each stem before its flower fades,
lift every labelled bulb to plant again,
and prune your trees and shrubs as each dictates.

I grow my plants so close they all complain
they've insufficient room to breathe, or sun
to drench their leaves, or share of summer rain,

let young weeds grow to be what they become,
and poppy stems and seed heads twist and dry –
then rot, when frost and winter rainfall come.

I watched you tend your silence constantly,
then found a careless way to nurture mine:
we've made our different landscapes home, and still

we touch each other's quiet awkwardly.
But looking now, when winter's worked its spell
of levelling, our gardens seem as one.

Spring terror

Snowdrops revert to merely green
when snow subverts their herald's role,
but thaw restores their callous poise
and sets in train an ebbing tide

which gathers speed like pressured steam
as each successive flower unfolds
and every longer day destroys
more of the darkness where we hide.

It quietly starts, and then it swells,
this growing distance from the shore –
and as my toes lose contact with

dissolving sand and broken shells,
I want to ask, beneath the roar,
has winter no more cold to give?

Place

But where shall wisdom be found?
And where is the place of understanding?
    – Job 28: 12

This garden breathes
as sunset strokes the goldenrod and slides away.

This place has known
the touch of raindrop, breeze and gale,
the sudden chill when crows call clouds –
the warmth when they disperse –
the breath of ghosts when breezes fail;

has felt the weight of ice
diminish, leaving
crumbled stone,
then heath, then grass, then trees;

has witnessed deer
then sheep, then horses graze,
lawns displace fields,
roads lead where paths once led,
to bivouacs, then barns, then homes;

has heard the sound of children's games,
of disputes, clashes, laughter,
campfires, kitchens, idling cars;
the quieter tones of love and tears,
and parents pointing out the stars;

has stood its ground,
as shadows marked the years and seasons by
the way they fell,
and waned or grew,
and when and where
they travelled from and to;

and now, as fading summer falls
on rose, anemone and goldenrod –
the gardener's pride –
if asked to weigh the worth of all it's held,
this gentle place would likely say
it could not tell.

Guelder rose

The undark night dissolves to deepest grey
there is no breeze – earth has no voice

two magpies swoop, then swerve away
and trains rush past in muffled silence

looming from, returning to
a stolen and dissembled light.

A blackbird's touch dislodges powdered snow –
the world's so vast, it's intimate.

A trace of sunken footprints threads the lawn
towards the guelder rose and where

your carefully tended garden's overgrown:
I find no hint of footprints there.

Empirical

'What if we had no why?'

Coronets of daffodils
have reappeared
beneath the willows
where they bloomed last year.

The nights and shadows shorten;
rivers chase
themselves toward the sea
in surging haste.

In chinks, blue sky drifts
soft rain clouds apart,
washed and adorned
with aquarelle and arc.

A song thrush lifts
and soars above the earth;
white blossom loosens, floats
from branch to turf.

I wake: before a moment
comes to pass,
know neither I,
nor what an I might ask,

nor even that this void's
a void, and then,
as blood to dust,
the fear of void seeps in.

What happened?

Had he discovered Christ's essential truth
when Luther nailed his theses to the door;

did Einstein's never-ending search for proof
elucidate a universal law;

or was it humble happenstance that saw
us tell their counting beads to gauge our worth?

Can gilding tales of nightly siege and war
they knew, dissolve our children's ingrained hurt?

Historians, parents, demagogues, the church,
our mischievous and guardian selves, TV...

make sense of all that's passed, on our behalf
but – never mind how well they choose their words –

by naming, they distort the shapes they see
and blur the backlit veil on which they're cast.

Execution

A thing I cannot reconcile,

as you were flung, and fell so fast –
yet drifted down so light and slow –

from rooftop under bluest sky
to meet the sudden square below:

I sat here merely, blinded by
low sunlight slanting through the rain and glass

The interview

Thank you for the question.
Yes, the shelling is more frequent today
and government troops are closing in.

We may not have the chance to speak again.

The unhidden thread

Grey sunlight glances off wet tarmac, boats
and barges surf and plough the wind and tide.
Planes fly above the cloud; from suburb, coast
and weald, the trains and buses flow in lines,

converge, and spill their riders to divide
and follow bridges, belts and stairways spread
about the city, footsteps synchronised –
all held in balance by a hidden thread.

I shiver from the beauty of this web,
and cower to foresense its fragile silk cut through –

in every instant see the river surge
with the pace and power of an untamed thoroughbred,

and render towers, gates and gold, and you,
grey-sunlit marshland overflown by birds.

Metro-man

These five stanzas can be read in any order, meaning there are 120 different poems here. Before reading, please assign a number to each stanza, from 1-5, at random, and read in that order. Then try again.

We snake like a slinky along the city's spine;
accelerate beneath the smiling metro-man
in fashionable jeans, who strides
the sky; then slow again to drop once more inside
the fume-blacked underpass; change gear
in thrall to the traffic flow we understand
no more of than our place within the line.
How did we come here?

We shuffle docile in an endless queue
to where security in caps and blazers nod
us grimly through their sacred arch.
Once in, through fields of electronic hum we march
to holy places we revere,
and where the luminosity of God
appears on tablets we pay homage to.
How did we come here?

From high, so high we barely hear the cars,
we gaze with chins on open palms, past sun-glazed towers
ordained in intricate array
towards untold horizons, where they fade away
in distant smog and disappear.
Daylight seems to sit with dark for hours,
then flees a nightscape of bright lights and bars.
How did we come here?

The traffic thins, and then we reach a place
where buildings end, the tarmac turns to roughened dirt,
the roadway narrows; looking back,
we're dwarfed by blank-eyed walls: uncertainly we track
a line of trees, and then with fear
we pass beneath their boughs, alert,
emerging into unfamiliar space.
How did we come here?

      We make love, we bury our parents, in concrete cells.
      Our living walls are desiccated; pictures do
      the work of trees, their canopies
      extend in a continuous and abstract frieze
      laid out by secret artists we're
      uncertain of, their tales of plants which grew
      before, a painful hint of what this life foretells.
      How did we come here?

Word was...

there were several ways
to reach beyond

you could
fly over, scale, vault
or tunnel beneath

or breach

or bring it down

or picture
marshlands and willows

wandering their wide
meander towards the distant sea

or simply walk
with the wall to your left or right

until the end

No guarantee

Overnight, the valley's turned.
Its trees and hedges, wearied by

the endless summer days, have spurned
their tender murmuring for dry-

as-paper rustling in reply
to breezes brushed with leaf more rare

than gold, beneath a cloudless sky –
a beauty he can hardly bear.

He sees leaves fade then fall; then bare
limbs silhouetted under rough

storm clouds; then spring – all he can know
is how their scent suffused the air,

the feel and soft sound as he scuffed
through dampened drifts, lifetimes ago.

Stet

On finding a group of ash trees, felled
to prevent the spread of disease.

Will children know the common ash,
will they infer what thing was here
from softened stumps, in future years
– like finding faded planting tags?

We claim the changes progress brings:
more choices, safer, longer lives –
but mourn the consequent demise
of quiet, starlight, hops, lapwings.

We've lived without the English elm;
we'll live without the ash, you say.
Perhaps. In my mind's eye I fell

each ash from every copse and field:
this leaves no wounds that scars can heal –
it drains the very light from day.

Arundel encampment

Stand, for a moment, cold,
beside the keep,
and the church whose broken walls
the wind blows through.

Look down the cobbled street that falls away
past doors whose shop-bells fail to ring,
to the riverside, where yours is the only car,
and cross the bridge,
to where the geometry of flint and brick and tarmac ends;

and the mystery of who decided where –
so sharply is it etched –
this town would terminate
and the fields be allowed to begin again;

and where,
among the tents
and right and pikes and muskets stacked in stooks,
in meadows bright in angled light,
the men who'd broken half the nave with cannon fire
and made of it a narrative,
then climbed and cleared the same steep street in rows,

returned
to speak a little, low,
addressing wounds against the background hum of busy work,
avoiding one another's eye, and – from this distance – yours,

and with their prayers cursed
both town and river bank
to never be free until
those rigid stooks no longer stand,
that never rust, nor fall, nor fade.

Buzzards

I hear her first – a screech half stolen by
the wind; then glimpse her lift away; flat tail,
white band along the underwing, as sail-
like storm clouds race behind. Again her cry

guides me towards first two, then three, and then
four buzzards, where there had been one, aloft
above the skylark field, adrift but deft
in their control of where the wind flew them.

Within a moment they have veered away
atop the gale; my spirit soaring free.
I've walked and worked this folded valley more

than thirty years; complained about the way
the world has changed, but never thought I'd see
four buzzards, where there had been none before.

Flax

...through generous fields of flax, their overlapping
flowers a gentle gentian; tangled mats
of chamomile among the wheat; to trapped-
in, hedged-in meadows, hemmed by sunken tracks
and spreading oaks, with you – so closer to
the past than I – I felt the touch of those
whose baulks of timber dragged these lanes, who knew
the cloying scent of mayweed, clover, drove
the horses pastured in these intimate
enclaves to till and sow. I wondered how
this path we trod began, saw William on
his horse lean forward to negotiate
his need: their right to walk and rent and plough
the land he'd won, with those he'd won it from.

Blackberries in Ukraine

The news tonight showed fighting in Ukraine.
  My eye was drawn, not to the scenes of war,
but swollen brambles glistening in the sun,
  in the hawthorn hedge behind the soldier's arm.

The camera didn't catch him quietly claim
  his harvest, but I somehow saw
his hand release the rifle, reach, and one
  by one dislodge the berries to his palm.

Though I can't wage his war, nor feel the pain
  his comrades, enemies and he endure,
I taste the same sharp juice which dyes his thumb
  and fingertips, and stains his uniform.

Were he to visit here, would what is strange
  or – as for me – familiar strike a chord?
In foreign fabric, does he see homespun:
  his world and mine lit by a single star?

Abroad, we introduce ourselves again
  to what we know; to where we've been before –
and hear the chorus crows and doves have sung
  at dawn since days began: discord and calm.

Perverse

The day we learned the Earth was doomed –
five years until the end –
we talked and talked the whole night through
and talked it through again,

and conjured plans for how we'd weave
new patterns in the past,
to reinvent today and cleave
our future from its path –

but then fell quiet as dawn revealed,
through misted glass, blurred views
of rooftops, roads and distant fields
we knew, and knew we'd lose,

and morning light diminished day,
extinguishing our fight,
while fog set in to shroud and weigh
upon five years of night –

through which we peered, saw no reprieve
but jagged, fire lit forms,
and children cowed, down on their knees
at barricades of thorns.

The floor above us creaked – we shared
an awful thought – a glance;
a child's soft foot fell on the stairs
and silence stopped our hearts.

We've planted trees, although we knew
they'd never be but young,
and raised our son and daughter to
be whom they might become.

Vast

for Barbara Hepworth

How did you know
before you reached inside and opened it,
the surfaces within a solid sphere would be

                                so vast
that light would brush their grain like fingertips
and never die?

How did you know
the only place to tilt and tap the blade;
how did you dare to make
the first – the final – cut?

How did you know
what we did not –
and would not, still:
our fear of seeing space unfolding endlessly?

Phil Vernon returned to the UK in 2004, after two decades in various parts of Africa. He lives in Kent, and works as an advisor on peacebuilding and international development. He mostly writes formal poetry, finding the interaction with pre-established patterns of rhythm and rhyme can lead in surprising directions. His poems have appeared in numerous magazines, journals and websites, and been shortlisted in competitions. A micro-collection, *This Quieter Shore*, was published by Hedgehog Poetry Press in 2018. His poetry website is www.philvernon.net/category/poetry.

HOW (NOT) TO GET YOUR POETRY PUBLISHED

HOW (NOT) TO GET YOUR POETRY PUBLISHED

Helena Nelson

HappenStance

First published in 2016
by HappenStance Press
21 Hatton Green, Glenrothes KY7 4SD
www.happenstancepress.com

Acknowledgements:
Thanks to the poets who have allowed me to use poems as a stimulus for
writing: Sue Butler, Jennifer Copley, Helen Evans, Charlotte Gann, Peter
Gilmour, Diana Gittins, Mark Halliday, Gill McEvoy, D.A. Prince, Stephen
Payne & Matthew Stewart. Andrew Waterhouse's poem 'Not an Ending'
is included with permission of Martin Waterhouse and Rialto Press; Tom
Duddy's 'Influenza' with permission of Sheila Duddy.

For sundry ideas and stimulus, thanks to Charlotte Gann, Marcia Menter,
Fiona Moore, J.O. Morgan, Alison Prince, Helen Tookey & Marion Tracy.
Warm thanks also to the proof-readers: Matt McGregor, Charlotte Gann,
Marcia Menter and Ross Kightly (Ross successfully defended the right
of personal and possessive pronouns not to be subdued to 'they/their'
domination.) All errors now present were inserted by Helena Nelson after
the proof-readers were done.

Note:
Some sections of this book appeared in an earlier incarnation either in a
2009 pamphlet with the same title or in the Happen*Stance* blog. The case
studies are fictitious, though similar situations occur in a publisher's life
on a regular basis.

The bright yellow cover features a large bold title, underneath which
there is a graphic of either a poet or editor groaning and tearing her hair,
much in the style of Olive Oyl in *Popeye*.

Printed and bound in the UK by 4edge Limited, Essex

ISBN 978-1-905939-97-8

CONTENTS

Foreword

Aprototype of this book was published as a pamphlet in 2009. It sold out quickly. Intended initially for 'new' poets in the UK, it turned out to be of interest to poets at all stages of their writing lives. I've been about to do a revised updated version ever since, but I've been too busy publishing poetry. In the meantime poetry publishing has grown even more complicated.

I found myself recently talking to a friend whose debut pamphlet appeared in 2014. We were discussing tactics for placing her first full collection, though she hasn't finished it yet. In the UK, publishers are usually working between two and four years ahead. For a poet with a successful, well-reviewed pamphlet published in 2014, if no offer for a book-length collection is in place by 2016 it could easily be 2018 before a book happens. Or longer. A 'successful' poet with poems widely appearing in top magazines could see a gap of five years between first pamphlet and first book.

I don't mean to sound depressing. I don't even think the situation is all *that* depressing. But in the discussion with my friend, I emphasised one thing – and it was this: when your proposal or manuscript lands on the publisher's desk they should recognise your name. That name, furthermore, should have overwhelmingly positive connotations. Whether the publisher will (or can) accept your work for publication is another matter, but the planning has to begin years before the manuscript goes in the mail.

This book deals with strategy. You may not think poetry and strategic planning have much in common, but why do you think some poets are successful in their publishing deals while others, who seem to you to write just as well, are not? Getting poetry published is a competitive game in which you create your own luck. The chapters that follow outline the necessary steps: the way you first present yourself as a poet; your networking on and offline; how to create a readership; the need to use the web intelligently; the business of 'track record'; the knack of thinking like a publisher; the thorny problem of self-promotion; and some advice on how to make your approach when you're finally ready.

I write both as a poetry publisher (HappenStance is based in Scotland and specialises in debut pamphlets and occasional books) and as a poet.

I have two full collections of my own in print at the time of writing, as well as self-published pamphlets. Some decades ago, I made all the painful mistakes a person could ever make. But there were so many things I didn't know! I truly thought all I had to do was write good poems and everything else would fall into place.

It seems to me now that the existence of the 'good poems' is almost the least of it when it comes to getting published (though also, in absolute terms, the only thing that matters).

Here's a confession. Twenty-five years ago I put a set of poems together and sent them to Faber & Faber, whose address I had found in the *Writers' & Artists' Year Book*. I had no idea of the poetry editor's name. I probably wrote 'Dear Sir/Madam'. Oh dear. Looking back on this now, the title of the collection strikes me as profoundly ironic: it was *The Disappointment Laundry*. When I packed off my baby in a fever of optimism, I had had perhaps two poems accepted for magazine publication in my entire life, neither of which I thought to mention in my covering letter. I nevertheless believed my work was excellent and was confident it would speak for itself. I was wrong on both counts. Of course the poems were returned (eventually). I knew something about poetry at that time, though not as much as I thought I knew. I had *no idea* how poetry publishing worked. I have learned a thing or two since. And in the last eleven years I have learned from the inside.

I hope the chapters that follow will prevent you from falling into the traps that detained me for some years and which I am usually now too embarrassed to mention. Or if you have already fallen victim to some of these errors, at least this book may help to explain what has gone wrong, and offer some new suggestions.

Should the poetry publishing challenge start to get you down, the book alternates planning chapters with practical writing exercises, ideas to engage the creative side of your brain, the bit that led you into the writing of poems in the first place. These are, of course, optional. You could skip them and just work on your five-year plan.

'Strategy' sounds like the contemporary workplace, and that's intentional. If you would like your work published at some point in the future, I suggest you regard getting published as a work task, though not without an element of playfulness. To reinforce that idea, there are workbook pages at the end of the volume.

Not only has publishing altered radically in the last two decades but it's still changing fast. (This is just as true for poetry as other genres.) Most of the poetry prizes continue to be won by the largest and most well-known imprints, but there are more small presses than there were, and new ones are always popping up. Many of these are publishing first collections, and some publish a dozen or so each year, though hardly any of these are shortlisted for awards.

Let's say – just theoretically – that 100 first collections per year are published in the UK. I feel certain that for each book-length collection accepted, over 100 are knocked back and those 100 rejected authors mainly have little idea why. In fact, it's not uncommon to find poets cherishing a sense of aggrieved injustice about their experiences. But sometimes we think in the wrong way, or ask the wrong questions. (There's also a chapter here on 'thinking outside the book' because sometimes if the game doesn't go your way, you need to change the game.)

It is possible, of course, that your poems are not 'there' yet. Making poems as good as they can be is the business of a lifetime. But I'm assuming yours are pretty good. And in that case they deserve the best chance of reaching some decent readers. I'm not surprised you're thinking about publication.

But first – how hard are you prepared to work at this? Because writing poetry is one job. A labour of love. An art.

Getting it published is quite another. 'Love' is not the key criterion. Think 'craft' rather than 'art' – with the emphasis on 'crafty'.

Chapter One: Why?

'Why do I write? I guess I've never felt the necessity of thinking up a really convincing answer to that one, although I get asked it a lot. I suppose I think it's a redundant question, like Why does the sun shine? As you say, it's a human activity. I think the real question is, Why doesn't everyone?'

—Margaret Atwood, in response to Joyce Carol Oates in 'Margaret Atwood: Poet', *New York Times on the Web*, May 21, 1978

QUESTIONS, QUESTIONS, QUESTIONS. 'Why do you write?' is one thing. 'Why do you want your poetry published?' is quite another. The fact that you're reading this book suggests you would like to see a collection of your work in print – or perhaps this has already happened and it didn't go well, or it was a long time ago. Or your last publisher has opted out. Or maybe you're thinking about this on behalf of someone else. A couple of times a year, as HappenStance editor, I'm approached by the relative of a poet who has died.

But why? There are all sorts of reasons for wanting to be published. I don't begin to suggest any of these is the 'right' one though some are better than others.

Let's start with that dead poet. When you lose a person you love and respect, publishing a book of their writing is a way of keeping part of them alive, or so it feels at the time. A sort of tribute.

Sometimes a poet has friends and family who believe the work is worthy of a wider audience. They tell the poet that he or she should get the poems published (though few realise how difficult this may prove). I remember my mother telling me I 'ought' to have a book published.

Or the poet may want to work in the field of creative writing, perhaps in a university, where it's essential to have publications to your name. He or she may already have completed an MLitt, or similar. The first poetry collection could be a necessary part of a career plan – among other things.

Or the poet could be a secret poet wanting to 'come out'. He or she has been scribbling for years but not telling anybody. So publication could be a way of publicly admitting commitment to the art.

Or the poet may want fame. John Keats certainly considered it a factor back in the nineteenth century.

Or the poet may have a burning desire to write on a specific subject, some key question to which he or she wants attention drawn. Perhaps it's part of a fund-raising exercise or central to a life's obsession. The need to publish may be urgent, and less about the individual poet than the cause itself.

Or the poet may want validation. Is the work any good? If it is, surely a publisher will accept and publish it. ('Have I been wasting my time all these years?')

Or the writer may want to make money. Some people are (wrongly) convinced their poetry will be commercially advantageous, both for themselves and the publisher. I keep a file of email approaches titled 'Mad Poets' because I'm fascinated by delusion. One poet estimated sales of 2000-5000 books for his poems. Another wrote, 'I WOULD LIKE TO SAY, THAT: IM A GENUINE GENIUS!' (though not, apparently, at punctuation). Another announced: 'I am a refreshing new talent'. One can't help admiring such enthusiasm and self-belief, though not perhaps enough to read the poems.

But there are more reasons yet. Poems need readers. Why else would you write them? So another good reason for publishing is to find readers. Publication gets the poems out there. You never know what connections could arise from this or what it could teach you.

On the other hand, some poets already have an audience. They are regular performers and their perfectly logical reason for publishing is to satisfy a demand.

Or the older poet may have served her or his time in the magazines, and have a body of work, but perhaps not an equivalent body of confidence. It's time to collect the work in book form, isn't it, before it's too late? It's what poets *do*.

Or perhaps the poet just wants the experience of publication, the learning experience. There's little doubt that making a book or a pamphlet of poems teaches you something about how poems do or don't hang together.

I'm sure there are more reasons I haven't thought of, perhaps almost as many as there are poets. But if you feel you want, or might want, a pamphlet or book of your poetry published, I suggest you reflect on what your reasons might be. Why? Because those reasons underpin your motivation.

You *can* get poetry published. There are many ways of doing it. It's not in the least impossible. But you will have to work at it. You'll need to invest time and probably cash too, in one way or another (no, I don't mean vanity publishing), and your reasons for wanting to be published will generate the motivation to keep you going when your confidence wears thin.

I don't think the search for fame is likely to keep you going for long. Or the belief that your poems will make money. But a combination of reasons may help you to use your intelligence and resourcefulness to find the way that's right for you. At the back of this book, in the workbook section, there's a 'Motivation' page to help you think this one through, if you haven't already done so.

To tell the truth, I find the topic of publishing both interesting and bothersome at the same time. Too much of it frankly gets me down. It's so easy to forget what the business of poetry is really about, which is writing POEMS. And writing poems is a thing that shouldn't be sullied. It's a private space, in which you do precisely what you want. You mustn't allow your writing self to be invaded by your getting-published self. The getting-published self deals with poems in the plural. The writing self is only interested in one thing: the poem in progress.

So between the publishing chapters of this book and the case studies, there are reading/writing stimuli. These are intended to engage the other, more joyous part of your brain. They may help remind you, should you happen to lose sight of it, what poetry is for. Of course, you could also ignore them and just read the 'how not to' bits. But really, despite any evidence to the contrary, this book is all about the poem.

Her Publisher

I love this time of year, time of day:
the light, pale-egg and misty; platform
almost empty. Malcolm says we'll wander,
find somewhere nice for lunch. We always do:
Italian spaghetti, a carafe
of red wine. I'll have to watch my frock.
I love all the bustle of Soho,
like another planet. The awards
don't start till 6. And, do you know, I don't
even mind meeting the Queen, the mood
I'm in. Plus I put the milk bottles out
already, and extra food for Saturn.

Malcolm's eyes are the colour of clear sky.
I'm sure to make the 11:03.

Charlotte Gann, from Noir, HappenStance 2017

W HAT DO YOU THINK of when you say 'publisher'? What sort
of person leaps into your mind? A man? A woman? Fat?
Thin? Young? Old?

Imagine you have one – your own personal publisher. A deal has
been agreed. You and s/he are going to meet. What will it be like? Write
the scenario. Call the poem 'My Publisher'.

When you've finished the scenario to your satisfaction, follow the
action at the bottom of this page but *don't read it yet.* That's why it's
upside down.

If you cheat, this won't work. Or perhaps it will, of course.

Cross out the title 'My Publisher'. Give the publisher another job altogether: a dark one.
Choose a new title. For example: My Undertaker. My Grave-digger. My Blackmailer. Or
similar . . . .

Chapter Two: How?

'. . . my proposal is that there should always be one minimum but essential requirement incumbent on publishers. And what is this indispensable minimum? That the publisher enjoys reading the books he publishes.'

—Roberto Calasso, *The Art of the Publisher*, Penguin Books 2015, tr. Richard Dixon

THERE IS A ROUTE that might be labelled 'traditional'. That is to say, it's the route many poets think they ought to follow, and some do still manage it. It's almost certainly not your route. However, it goes something like this.

The poet is keen on poetry from a young age, and probably keen on writing in general. He or she reads poetry and maybe has had some poems in a school magazine. An enthusiastic English teacher or influential parent may play a role.

The poet may win something when young: a school prize for poetry, or maybe a Foyle Young Poets prize, or something like that.

The poet leaves school and usually goes to university (yes, UK poetry is dominated by writers with a degree or so to their name). She or he may study English, but actually any subject will do so long as the poet keeps writing poems. By now, that young writer has clocked the idea that there's a 'scene'. She or he may go to poetry events, readings, festivals etc., send poems to worthy magazines and some will be accepted. The poet may get involved with a literary magazine as an editor or a founder. She or he may have a mentor.

By 'mentor' I mean someone who knows the poetry ropes, and takes an interest in the young person. Someone who encourages the young person to believe in their gift. A critical friend. (These days there are also formal mentorship schemes, but I'll come to those later.)

Between the years of 19-21, the young poet is placing poems in medium quality magazines, has made some friends in Poetry World – met some editors, hung out with published poets, been to events here and there, read swathes of contemporary writing. So this writer is working at it, no question, whatever else she or he is doing.

The young person may also have a slightly unusual background: perhaps she or he is also gifted in another way – at music, or maths, or physics, or gymnastics. Or something has characterised her or his life – travel, or tragedy, or speaking five languages, or having a father who runs a zoo or a mother who runs a circus. This unusual background leaks into the poems and makes them a little different in terms of focus and content.

And this young poet is strongly 'driven', considering approaching a pamphlet publisher, or entering one of the pamphlet competitions. She or he may enter a couple of times, fail to win, and then take the challenge more seriously. She or he may be able to afford to go on an Arvon Course for a kick-start. Or she or he may participate in a good quality writing workshop.

By 23-25, the young scribbler will have got a pamphlet into print and started doing readings at various poetry events. This poet's name will be … out there. The sort of name you've heard because the poems seem to be all over the place, whether or not you enjoy reading them. She or he will have poetry friends in the same age group. They will help each other.

The young poet may also have placed poems in anthologies, may have attracted a bit of attention with something unusual or controversial, may have begun to write reviews of other people's work. Before he or she is thirty, this writer will win an Eric Gregory Award. In order to win such an award, the poet knows his/her way around Poetry World and has sufficient self-belief and ambition to apply. The young poet has also a sound body of work to her or his credit.

In fact, this young poet knows quite a lot not only about poetry but how poetry publishing works. He or she has met, in person, some of the main editors from the biggest poetry imprints. He or she may even have talked to one of them at length on some poetry course where the editor is a tutor. In conversation one day in a pub or other hostelry, the publisher/editor says, 'You must send me some of your work.' The young poet does so.

The publisher/editor reads the poems and enjoys them. The publisher likes the idea of this young, edgy, intelligent poet who presents as radical or beautiful or Irish or dangerous or unusually scientific or prolific in Arabic or working in a diamond mine or sailing single-handed round the world or . . . whatever. Here we have an author of talent, with durability and development potential. A poet who looks worth investing in.

So the publisher offers to bring out a debut collection. The book duly appears and is shortlisted for at least one of the first-collection prizes. That poet is on her or his way to where time alone (and perhaps eventually posterity) will tell.

Dear reader, I don't know what age you are, but it's possible that you're already long past the possibility of being this young poet-person. Many poets these days don't even start writing until they've lived a half century or so. So it well may be that this route is already ruled out for you. Or that you did it all thirty years ago, failed at one of the necessary hurdles and gave up for half a lifetime. It happens.

But many poets follow *part* of this path. That is to say, they do their time. They read. They take note. They learn. They place poems successfully in a range of magazines. They join a writers' group. They participate in readings/events. They have a degree of success and are encouraged to believe they have a body of work that merits publication in pamphlet or book form.

Let's go with that for the moment.

Case Study

The post arrives: three new sets of poetry. Two are nonstarters, but the third is interesting. It's a lovely submission from a poet who is also a photographer. Each poem is matched to a gorgeous full colour photograph and the connections are vivid and interesting.

There's only one problem. I don't print in colour, and I don't print illustrated booklets, not even in black and white. I don't have that kind of budget.

This is a poet who has found out enough about my imprint to know I publish pamphlets, but hasn't checked out their format or house-style. A sounding-out letter or email would have saved him some time, not to mention £4.38 in postage.

Write now: The wayward pen

'Such words as 'inspiration' and 'talent' are bandied about, emphasising the supposed difference between these and 'ordinary' people. This is an entirely artificial division. The flowering of creativity takes place in small acts all the time; in a question asked at a public meeting or the writing of a letter to a friend or even in such trivial-seeming matters as complaining about a dirty glass in a pub.'

—Alison Prince, from *The Necessary Goat & Other Essays on Formative Thinking*, Taranis Books, 1992

I N THIS BOOK, THE pages about publishing alternate with writing ideas because I'm assuming you're a poet, and planning how to get published can drive you daft if you think about it uninterruptedly. Also I happen to think writing is a magical thing and good for us all. But of course the writing ideas are optional and you may have better ones of your own.

This one is a little tricky. You need to find a writing implement you don't normally use and aren't particularly comfortable with. You might even need to buy one on purpose. Or steal it: stolen pens are particularly good for this exercise. (Stealing someone else's poem is plagiarism, stealing their pen is merely theft.)

But this writing implement shouldn't look or feel like anything you would ordinarily use. It must, however, write easily. The ink should flow well, the pencil should be sharpened and not the kind that breaks all the time.

Once you've chosen the writing implement put it somewhere you can see it. The correct emotion you should have when you look at it is suspicion. Leave it for at least a day and a night.

The writing implement is now charged. I mean this in the sense of an electric charge. It has an energy and purpose of its own.

So far, so good.

Now take a look at Stephen Payne's poem on the next page.

Dyslexia

A hard thing to explain to an eight-year-old.
How to lift from everything we know
a clutch of truths by which he'll be consoled.
I keep to what it doesn't mean, name
the famous cases. Hard to answer no
when he asks quietly, Are you the same?

Stephen Payne, from Pattern Beyond Chance, HappenStance 2015

It's a poem on a difficult topic, isn't it? It doesn't console, though many poems do. Even the darkest poems *can* reassure – because we've survived to write them, if nothing else. Your turn now. Pick up the charged writing implement and write.

The instrument in your hand is determined to write about something you don't want to write about at all. I have no idea what that thing might be, only that you *really* don't want to write about this, whatever it is.

Let the pen have its way. Write until the energy is exhausted and the pen is just another pen. Put the piece of writing away.

When you come back to it, you have a choice. You can destroy the piece of writing (burn it) and write about the act of writing it, the act of being subservient to the pen.

Or you can edit with another pen, or even a word processor, because you're never going to write with that implement again. Throw it away. Give it away. Give it back. Whatever. Its job is done.

Chapter Three: Which publisher, and are you ready?

'... the literary publisher may occasionally be tempted by the commercial title in the hope of replenishing his bank balance and the commercial publisher may always be tempted by a literary title, since aspiring to prestige is a weed that grows everywhere.'

—Roberto Calasso, *The Art of the Publisher*, Penguin Books 2015, tr. Richard Dixon

I'VE BEEN REFERRING MERRILY to 'getting poetry published' and suggesting 'publishers' are all members of the same family. They're not. They're dramatically different from each other. The only thing they have in common is publications with poems in them.

Some poetry publishers have higher status than others. At the time of writing, the so-called 'big five' are Bloodaxe, Random House Group (includes Cape; Vintage; Chatto & Windus), Carcanet, Faber & Faber and Picador. Only two of these publish solely poetry (Bloodaxe and Carcanet). The prestigious UK poetry prizes are usually (there are rare exceptions) won by collections from these publishing houses. This could mean they publish the best poetry of our era. This could mean they are the only publishers worth approaching, if fame and success are your goals.

But assume nothing. There are many kinds of 'success'. The world of poetry is far more full of opinions, blurb and hype than facts. The only true success for a poet is writing at least one good poem.

Getting work published is not the same as writing good poems. Writing poetry and continuing to learn about that craft is the work of a lifetime. Finding the right publisher or editor can assist that process. Finding the wrong one means you're on your own. Or worse – praised where you should be challenged. In the meantime a lot of dodgy advice is floating about. Recently an aspiring poet I know was told by a worthy mentor: 'Send your manuscript to at least ten publishers at once'.

The key (to my mind) is not how *many* publishers you send to but which ones you choose to approach, and why. But let me backpedal slightly. Supposing you *did* decide to send your collection of poems to ten publishers, where would you start? If you were to look at the The Poetry Library (Southbank Centre) website, you'd find a handy list. At the time of writing it comprises 123 publishers. (There are more than this: my list of poetry pamphlet publishers alone numbers 90 at the time of writing.) Each has contact details, together with a paragraph telling you something about preferences. The first of these reads as follows:

> 'Acumen Publishing produces one to two books and three pamphlets a year. These are 95% by invitation to poets whose work has greatly appealed in the magazine *Acumen*. The pamphlets are for promising poets of all ages who have had no collected publication previously.'

So if you're considering Acumen, and you've never had a poem in *Acumen* magazine, cross that option off your list. But if you *have* had poems in *Acumen*, it's not necessarily the place to start either. If the editor was bursting to publish your first pamphlet, you might have had an 'invitation' by now. Besides, you need to get hold of a few Acumen poetry pamphlets. Do you like them? Is this the sort of publication you're hoping for?

Most people hoping to have work published find their way to the current addresses of publishers via one route or another. They can be found on more than one website, as well as inside library reference books such as *The Writers and Artists Yearbook*, or *The Writer's Handbook*.

So this is what some poets do next, first in your list of things *not* to do. They click on, or type out, the email address (often without even reading the paragraph of information carefully) and send a message to the publisher. As Happen*Stance* editor, I had two such emails only last week (from separate poets). They read something like this:

```
Dear Editor

I have a collection of poems I would like
to get published. Please tell me something
about your preferences so I know whether it
is worth sending to you.

Yours sincerely

Doug Wright
```

```
Dear Sir or Madam:

I am interested in publishing my collection
of poems provisionally titled The Hearts
and Minds of Oceans. Could you tell me
something about what kind of poetry you
```

usually prefer? Some of my poems have
violent or sexual content that might not be
to everyone's taste.

You will be able to read a selection of my
poems at my website: www.AmazingAmanda.com.
Please take a look and let me know if you
are interested. Thank you for your time.

Amanda Aberystwyth-Perkins
Amy@AmazingAmanda.com

These emails were a waste of time for their authors. Why? Because all they've done is reveal ignorance and apparent laziness. The writers haven't bothered to find the name of the editor (in the age of the internet, this is child's play). And there's no point asking a publisher what he or she prefers. It simply shows you know nothing about their publishing record and current list of poets.

Worse still, the author of the second example has an extremely memorable name (though in this case fictional). So that means if Amanda Aberystwyth-Perkins makes another, more carefully prepared, approach in the future, she'll be remembered as Amazing Amanda who sent an email without finding the name of the editor or knowing anything about the imprint.

But I'm sure you're better prepared than this. You may even be looking for someone to take on your second book. You will need to present yourself to the publisher as a viable proposition. Are you in a position to do this? It's useful to do a swift self-appraisal of your 'success' so far (see also workbook pages 124-126.)

1. List at least six paper magazines that have printed your work in the last three years.

2. If you have publications already in print (books, pamphlets), note them down.

3. If you have had poems in anthologies, list the books in which they appear, with publication dates.

4. Does your work appear on the web? If so, where? List sites, including your own, if applicable.

5. Have you won or placed in any poetry competitions? If so, list your triumphs, with dates.

Right. That's a brief overview of your public self. I have asked you to list magazines that have published your work. I haven't asked you to consider how much kudos they carry. But it isn't rocket science to work out which are most prestigious. The top journals often pay authors for publication – I mean actual *money*. They're also costly to subscribe to and usually have some public funding.

Online, the most desirable ezines publish well-known poets, so look for names you recognise. Another way to work out which publications carry clout is to look inside the debut books of recent first collection prize-winners and see which magazines they acknowledge. It's likely they've been placing their poems judiciously. Watch and take note.

Now – more questions to test your readiness.

1. What are the names of the (poetry) editors of the following presses? Bloodaxe Books, Faber & Faber, Cinnamon, Carcanet, Picador, Liverpool University Press (Pavilion Poetry), Cape, Seren, Nine Arches, Indigo Dreams.

2. List the names of five poetry pamphlet imprints (book publishers mentioned above are excluded from this list)?

3. Name ten poetry collections (books or pamphlets) you've read in the last two years, and say who the publisher was for each one.

Okay. How did you get on? If you found it hard to answer these questions, I suggest there's some way to go before you can approach a publisher, and I haven't yet started on the research required (see Chapter 5). You need an informed understanding of who does what and where before you can enter the fray with a decent chance of success.

If you answered most of my questions fairly easily, well done. But it's about to get harder. Here's the bottom line: in order to get a collection of poetry published with a reputable publisher (like every other aspect of life there are exceptions) you must already have placed poems widely, in well-regarded outlets.

If you're looking for a book-length collection, it would be an advantage to have already published at least one pamphlet that was well reviewed and sold well. This would suggest you've already created at least a small readership. Some experience of public reading (again with some good feedback) would also be advantageous.

You *don't* have to have won any competitions, though it's nice if you have.

You *don't* need to be rich.

You *don't* need endorsements from well-known poets, especially not well-known poets who write endorsements for lots of people.

You *don't* have to have your own website.

But you *do* need to know your way around the world wide web. You *do* need to use email. You need to be able to say the word 'internet' without groaning. Why? It's in chapter five.

But first, there's the issue of the magazines. Why do you need to get poems in magazines? Why can't they just go straight into a book?

Case Study

A submission arrives accompanied by a very nice letter. The poet mentions two of my recent publications – in fact I remember her name because she ordered them a couple of months ago online. I'm delighted she enjoyed Tom Duddy – and especially 'Side Street'. She doesn't seem to have checked my website for submission guidelines though.

She has enclosed a full pamphlet collection: twenty-five poems *stapled* together with a contents page and front cover. She's offering me *The Barren Field*, a set of poems about the loss of her husband. Hm. I wonder. I've just published a pamphlet focussing on the death of a sister. Is it too soon for me to do another publication similar in theme? Probably.

But her magazine track record is not bad. And poems about death aren't always about death.

Let's take a look at the work. The first three pages put me off: too much overt emotion splashing around. But I like the next four very much – they're light and uplifting. Normally I would pick out these four and put them on the top of the pile, while I think about the rest. I can't do that in this case because of the wretched staples, so I start to feel irritable. I hate it when they bind the pages together. Why do I have submission guidelines if nobody bothers to read them?

Still here

My father stands in the garden.
The dead have left him behind.
He's holding his shopping-bag full of framed photographs.
Mum looks up at me, a crack across her chin.

How am I going to cater for him now?
He won't eat my cauliflower cheese, my gravy-less dinners.
Nothing like hers, he'll say,
sticking the knife in.

He still has his soul. It appears no one else wants it.
It's fluttering in his chest like a dodgy heartbeat,
like ginger shortbread bubbling in the oven.

Jennifer Copley, from *Living Daylights*, Happen*Stance* 2011

THINK OF SOMEONE WHO'S gone. Someone who isn't alive any more, or at least you've lost them completely: someone you miss. Bring them back.

Write about them as though they're right here beside you doing whatever they do. Imagine them back into existence.

You might write a conversation between you and them. Or you might simply say what you're doing, and what they're doing. You're writing a poem. They're looking out through the window saying, 'Is dinner ready yet?' And so on.

At the end of the poem, the missing person leaves.

Chapter Four: Sending poems to magazines

'I began the Horse as a forum for the best writing about poetry and the best poetry (by my own lights) I could find: the public flip-side to my own writing. That is still how I see it: each issue as, in a way, a large poem, put together with all the care one can muster: a gathering of poets and critics writing as passionately and genuinely in or about this art as they can – an art which, as Patrick Kavanagh said, you dabble in and find has become your life.'

—Gerry Cambridge, editorial to the 20th anniversary issue of *The Dark Horse*, 2015.

I'M ALWAYS TELLING POETS to get on with 'the business', send the poems out, get them into the best magazines they can. Why? There are poets who leap into book publication without a previous 'track record', but it's rare. I like the magazine (and sometimes ezine) route. Why would a publisher like this kind of 'track record'? There are a number of reasons. Here are ten for starters.

1. Peer validation. If a prospective publisher suspects your poems are good, they like to have this confirmed by other editors. (It sometimes happens that poems I think are brilliant *don't* get into good magazines, but it's unusual). Also publishers *do* read magazines and notice the poets in them and nod, and even occasionally note down a name. But this is not the most important of the reasons.

2. Once printed in a magazine, the poems are out there finding readers, which is the independent life every poem deserves. Someone, somewhere is sitting up in a chair astonished, and thinking *Good grief! What a poem!* That's one reader. Two readers thinking the same is a readership.

3. In magazines, the poet's name is bobbing around gathering momentum and recognition. We buy or borrow books (eventually) written by people we've heard of, not people whose names mean nothing to us. So if you find a publisher to produce your book, this magazine track record will help it sell. Eventually.

4. The magazine-submitting poet is a member of the community of jobbing poets. It's part of the apprenticeship, if you like. It's an honourable striving. If the poems aren't accepted, the effort is no less praiseworthy. Besides, you're going to stick at it. You're going to send them somewhere else, aren't you? And if they come

back rejected, you can add another slip to your rejection collection. More importantly, you can take another look at that poem. Is the title right? Does each line fall exactly as you want it? Make a change if necessary. If not, have faith. Send the poem out again, to another editor.

5. When you *do* have a poem accepted, soon you find yourself between the covers of the magazine with other poets. You read their work carefully then, especially the one on the facing page. You feel almost as though you've met that poet in person. And sometimes you do. You go to a magazine launch and blimey – there you are sitting next to your facing-page poet. It's a bond that can last, with luck, a lifetime.

6. Most magazines (not all) have a bit of biographical detail about authors. If a publisher has offered to do a collection for you next year, you can flag this in the bio. It's another tiny cog in the great wheel of promotion.

7. Once your book or pamphlet of poems is accepted for publication, you want the book reviewed as warmly and widely as possible. Magazines that run reviews (not all of them do) will often review poets whose work they've previously published. If they haven't published your poems (unless your publication is prize-winning or PBS-recommended) you can usually forget being reviewed. Reviews don't sell many books, but they're still another element in promotion of your book and your publisher's brand.

8. Just as a magazine is a creative work made by the editor(s), so a publishing imprint is a creation, and the proud creator wants it to be well-regarded. A good reputation brings the best poets and the best poets strengthen the reputation. Each time one of 'my' poets has work in a leading magazine and the bio name-checks HappenStance, the imprint's reputation is enhanced.

9. Your first collection is in print. You are still, aren't you, the jobbing poet, stalwartly sending poems out to the magazines? Someone reads your latest sestina in a magazine and loves it. They look up the bio. They see you have a book in print. They buy it!

10. It's hard graft, this regular sending out of poems, but it strengthens you. Certainly rejection of your favourites can be demoralising. But there are at least three key aspects to the poetry business. The

first is the best – the making of poems, the joy, excitement and fun of that. Second is getting those poems as good as they can be, which means exposing them to strangers. The third thing is determination. Stickability. Doing the necessary business of sending them out, filing the returns. Earning respect because you don't give up. Standing up and being counted. You wanna be a poet? This is your job.

Case Study

A nice looking set of poems arrives during my reading window. They're well-presented and the author writes a good covering letter. She is most amusing about her life time of breeding dogs – golden retrievers. (As it happens, golden retrievers are my favourite dogs.)

She tells me she wrote poetry in her teens and early twenties, but stopped when she had a family. She returned to it when she lost her husband five years ago in a car crash. Poetry has sustained her through some bad times, she has written quite a lot, and is confident she now has enough poems for a strong pamphlet.

She has only just started sending poems out, she says, but she has about 40 that are 'ready'. Three have already appeared in *Lycetta* (not a great magazine but a good place to start). Twenty others are under consideration with *Poetry Review, The Rialto, Poetry Wales, Wasafiri, Magma* and *Stand*. For a moment, the names of these magazines catch my eye – and I'm impressed. Then I realise by 'under consideration' she means they haven't been rejected yet.

I take a quick look at the poems. There's good potential but I think some way to go: there are weaknesses in construction and too many of them follow a similar shape and form. But one of them is *very* interesting, and I put two more to one side to think about later. I suspect, like many poets, she's trying to move too fast. For her, five years is a long time. For me, it seems remarkably short.

01252 722698

You worked your way round my milk teeth,
sung umpteen times before you stuck.
Soon a chameleonic code,
you were my safeguard from a snatch,
then my duty when staying out,
and recently a thankful leap
from trade fairs and dogged insects.
My fingers refuse to leave you.

Matthew Stewart, from *Inventing Truth*, HappenStance 2011

YOU OFTEN HEAR THE phrase: 'The statistics speak for themselves.' So let them have their say.

Or maybe think about numbers in your life in general and where they have resonance. Do they have colours for you? (Some people are synaesthetic with numbers as well as letters.) Or are they hard to visualise? I can remember my grandmother's Co-op membership number by rhythm. It stuck in my head like a rhyme when I was about eight and has stayed there for over half a century.

Of course, 'Numbers' is also an old word for poetic measure. Alexander Pope famously says in 'An Epistle to Arbuthnot':

As yet a child, nor yet a fool to fame,
I lisp'd in numbers, for the numbers came.

If you look carefully at Matthew Stewart's poem you'll see he's not using metrical numbers but syllabic measures: eight lines with eight syllables for each, the whole thing 64 syllables. And what a lovely last line!

So try starting with numbers. Let them come into your head – familiar numbers that are there already, and then whatever they connect with. When you start to write, use a syllabic count to dictate your line length. As many lines in total as each line has in syllables. Play about with this. See what happens.

Chapter Five: Making the web work for you

'... no one has ever been plucked from obscurity by a publisher, inexperienced and ignorant of the poetry scene, its operations, its bias, indeed its enmities, hostilities and prize-fixing glamour, and succeeded to achieve marvellous book sales. Knowing the scene (and being known by it) and establishing your relationship to it are as important as scribbling vers libre in the attic, or work-shopping quatrains at the weekend writing school.'

—Chris Hamilton-Emery, *101 Ways to Make Poems Sell*, Salt Publishing 2006.

CAN YOU IMAGINE A nineteenth century poet who refused to use the postal service? A person who was prepared to talk to people but not write to them? A writer who wouldn't use the main means of written communication?

If you don't engage with the internet, you can be a perfectly sane person (perhaps saner than the rest of us). You can be writing brilliant poems. But you're out of touch with the main means of communication in the twenty-first century. I still receive letters and submissions from poets who don't use the net at all, some of them not even for email. Others have a token email address, but do they use it? Hardly ever. A big bit of me admires determined resistance to technology. But as a publisher, I can't afford to be like that. If you're determinedly web-resistant, you should skip this chapter and go on to other ways of building a readership. But for most aspiring poets, the web is a necessary evil, and frequently a necessary good.

This week, at the time of writing, poet Gerry Cambridge, whose work I publish, is taking part in a live online reading. It's a transatlantic reading. The other poet-participant is David Mason in Colorado. This is a free event, organised through the Scottish Poetry Library. Anybody can 'go'. Anybody with access to the web, that is. Poets need access to the web. I know of at least two other poetry readings this very night that are *not* on the web. They're in pubs. You need both.

Before the internet existed, you had to go to a library or bookshop to find out about publishers in resources like the *Writers and Artists Year-book*, or the *Writers' Handbook*. These books still exist and contain much useful information. But when it comes to researching your publisher, submission guidelines on the net are easy to find, more detailed, and more likely to be up to date. (I update mine every six months.)

If you haven't done this already, go to the websites of at least five poetry presses and look for 'submission guidelines'. If you don't know the address (URL) for each one, google them by name. Some publishers make this easier than others. If you don't know where to start, I recommend you go to Bloodaxe (www.bloodaxebooks.com). Look at the header along the top of the home page. Click on the tab that says 'Contact'. At the time of writing, this will take you to 'Submissions'.

But on the website of every publisher there will be similar information somewhere. Sometimes the tab says 'Submissions', sometimes it's under 'About' or 'Contact' or FAQs. It doesn't normally take too long to track it down, though you don't find it immediately. Why? The first aim of the publisher's website is to *sell* books, not buy them. You want them to *buy* a book – your own – though you may not have thought about it in this way. You want them to spend a great deal on you – not just £9.99, the cost of one book, but many hundreds of pounds invested in reading, editing, print costs, marketing resources and time.

As I said in chapter three, poets are sometimes advised to send a manuscript to as many as ten publishers at once. I would not do this, for a variety of reasons. At the time of writing, the Carcanet Press submissions page (which you find by clicking on 'Information') provides a link to an interview with managing editor Michael Schmidt. Here's what Michael has to say on the topic of 'simultaneous submissions':

> 'We're very much against it. Reading a manuscript is an investment of time and effort, and if you really like it, the last thing you want to find out is that someone else has offered on it as well. We're not rich enough to enter bidding wars. So we always think that if poets submit their work to Carcanet, it's because they want to be published by Carcanet and not someone else.'

Let me tell you this: all publishers want to think the poet is submitting to them because they want to be published by that publisher. They all want to be the first choice of a brilliant and dedicated poet. So whether or not this is true, you need to persuade them it is.

But why would you want to be published by Carcanet, and not Faber? Or Red Squirrel and not Cultured Llama? Or Shoestring and not

Greenwich Exchange? After all, it's more than likely none of them will consider publishing your work. Before you try to convince them to be interested in *you*, you had better decide why you're interested in *them*. So find out all you can. Follow them on Twitter. Set up a Google alert for the poetry editor's name. If what I'm saying sounds like a foreign language, don't feel inadequate. Your language is poetry, not Twitter or Instagram. It isn't true that the most successful poets are internet experts. But you have to start somewhere, and you'll be surprised how quickly you learn, especially if you make contact with other poets, some of whom will be better at it than you. They will help you.

However, researching publishers thoroughly is time-consuming because there's a huge amount of information out there. It's not just the publisher's website you need to check: you should be able to track down interviews, features and possibly even filmed discussions in which they took part. Treat this like your specialist subject on *Mastermind*. It's a research project, not ten minute gallop round Google, and ideally you have more than one publisher in mind. Let's review how far you've got.

1. In your notebook (or use workbook page 127) list three poetry publishers you think you might approach, in order of preference.

2. Next to the name of each of these three, explain why you selected them. (Good reasons, mind. You're not allowed to write next to Faber & Faber 'because they are so well known'!)

If you find it hard coming up with convincing reasons, or can't see the difference between one publisher and another, your next task is obvious. Find out as much as humanly possible about the three you listed. Put your web research to the test. Here are some questions you might try answering (see also pages 128-130).

1. What's the poetry editor's name?
2. Is the editor also a poet or a reviewer? If so what has s/he published? Have you read any of it?
3. How long has the publisher been in business? Age? Background?
4. Does the editor select from open submission, or are they chosen through a competition process? Or other means?
5. Have any publications from this press in the last two years been

shortlisted for prizes? If so, what?

6. How many poetry books do they publish each year?

7. If you want a *first* collection published, how many debuts did they publish last year?

8. Can you tell anything about the range of poetry they publish – mainstream/performance/innovative/experimental? paper books/e-books? (Do you know how your own work might be categorised?)

9. Are any recent books by this publisher reviewed online or anywhere you can read the reviews? Read them.

10. Look in the acknowledgements and bio sections of the books you've found from this publisher: can you deduce anything about track record & background of the poet?

11. How's the publisher funded? How stable is the enterprise? Does it look like they'll keep going for the next few years?

12. Have they published any poetry you like a lot? What?

13. Track down some of the books as physical objects. What's the production quality like? Do you like what you hold in your hand?

14. Are there any online interviews or blog entries from the editor that might provide useful background?

15. How does this publisher promote and sell the books?

16. Do you know any poets published by this publisher who would talk to you about how it all came about and what their experience was like?

17. Does the publisher have a house magazine?

What do I mean by a 'house magazine'? Some publishers print a regular poetry journal as well as books, like Acumen Publications with *Acumen* magazine. On the Carcanet submissions page you'll see information about sending poems to *P.N.Review*. Nine Arches Press has *Under the Radar*, Cinnamon Press has *Envoi*. Templar Poetry publishes *Iota*; Diehard Publishing brings out *Poetry Scotland*. So if you're thinking of approaching Carcanet about a book-length manuscript, first send poems to *P.N.Review*. If a couple of attempts with poems elicit no interest, consider another publisher.

But I suggest you don't approach a publisher at all unless you've found the answers to most of my list of questions. You *must* have read some of the books they've recently published or, if you're using the web to your advantage, you may be able to read selected pages on Amazon free. You need to admire what they do and want to be part of it – genuinely. You need to know as much about them as you can. They are unlikely to be interested in you unless you're interested in them.

Yes, I know this will take ages. Writing poetry's a serious business. Getting it published is another serious business. It may not be joyful and creative, but it's most interesting. And it's something you can use your intelligence to plan and prepare – with an amazingly rich resource to help you: the internet.

Now for the other use of the world wide web – the more scary side – to let the world know something about *you*. But first, a bit of writing.

Case Study

A letter from a poet friend arrives. She has just had a reply from a small publisher to whom she sent a full collection of poems a few months ago. The publisher says she likes the work and thinks it would make a good book but notes the author does not appear to have an email address. All authors for this imprint are required to be contactable by email.

The friend has resisted the online world so far but as a result of this letter, she has just enrolled in a class called 'Surviving the Internet for the Terrified.'

She promises me her next communication will be by email. She has installed a broadband connection and bought a laptop. Her nephew is coming to make sure everything works right next week. Do I think she she has left this all too late? And is it *really* true one can't get poetry published without an email address?

Of course it's not too late. She'll be fine, although we have corresponded on paper with pen and ink for a very long time and I hope that won't stop.

I have never told a poet they couldn't get poetry published without an email address, but I do wonder how I would manage all the communication about proofs and changes and flyers and web pages without it.

Write now: The tools of your trade

'All genuine creativity centres round the effort to identify the truth of an experience.'

—Alison Prince, from *The Necessary Goat & Other Essays
on Formative Thinking*, Taranis Books, 1992

HAVE YOU GOT A trade with a language of its own? I don't mean plumbing or electrical work, though these would do nicely. I mean any occupation that generates specialist vocabulary.

If you're a gardener, you use gardening terms. You talk about 'pricking out' and 'thinning' and 'hardy annuals' and you know what you mean. Or maybe you love making curries: think of the names of your favourite spices and cooking methods. Or a photographer. Or a musician. Or possibly you're unwell: if you get ill with something that has a name, soon you know all its special terms, its drug names, its treatment names.

I have no idea what your area of expertise may be, but I'm willing to bet you have one. I once worked with a group on a confidence-building course, and each person in the group (they were all women) had to write down one skill she *knew* she had. One woman shook her head blankly. 'I'm not good at anything,' she said. 'Yes you are,' I said. 'Think harder.' So she wrote down, 'Hoovering.' At that time, the Japanese best-seller *The Life-Changing Magic of Tidying* by Marie Kondo had not been written, and neither had Kim and Aggie starred in *How Clean Is Your House* on Channel 4. There's nothing wrong with hoovering and not everybody is good at it.

Everybody has expertise at *something*. Almost always, that thing – whatever it is – has a vocabulary of its own. People who speak such a language don't value it, because to them it's an everyday practical thing. But language that belongs to a territory is magical. Take it out of its home country and it will do things you don't expect.

This writing exercise challenges you to describe a 'trade' activity in the language that belongs to it. Just describe it, like an instruction manual, but take care to put in the words that belong precisely to this activity.

Now take a look at what you've got. How transferable is it? You may need to make a few tweaks. You might like to reflect on the possibility that at some level every poem, among its other concerns, is about the act of writing poems. Here's an example from Helen Evans' debut pamphlet, *Only By Flying* (HappenStance, 2015). Helen is a glider pilot, among other things.

Pre Take-Off Checks

Controls: Are your rudder and ailerons
connected and working properly? Are you sure
you have full and free movement?

Ballast: Do you need more?
Or are you already carrying too much?

Straps: Will you be held securely during spins,
rolls, tail slides, high-speed stalls, loops,
and any unforeseen manoeuvres?

Instruments: Do they read accurately?
Are your batteries charged and running?
Will you select QNH or QFE?

Flaps: Are you confident coping with flaps?

Trim: Have you picked the correct attitude?

Canopy: Is your vision unobstructed?
Have you located the red emergency-jettison lever?
Could you bale out if you had to?

Brakes: Can you open them fully?
And are they closed and locked?

Eventualities: Are conditions suitable for flying?
Is the windsock lying?
If the launch fails, what will you do?

Chapter Six: Social networking for poets

Most people surely ignore most hype. I think there's a turning away from the social media – not a backlash, more a sort of weariness, a lowering of the decibels, a shrug.

—Charles Boyle, SonofaBook blog, May 2015

MANY WRITERS ARE NATURALLY private people. They're don't jump on bandwagons and they're rightly wary of what they say in print. So why would they join networks like LinkedIn and Facebook and Twitter and Pinterest?

You can take part in social networking without using any of these networks. When you exchange emails with poetry friends, that's precisely what you're doing. When you join a private online writing group with its own discussion board, you're networking.

But there are some advantages to having a presence on the bigger social networks, provided you're careful. I often think these networks are like a gigantic school playground. You don't just march in there and start a game of football. You hang about and see how it works, and make a few friends who've been there longer than you have. On social networks you can be what is often called a 'lurker'. That is to say, you watch what's going on but you don't take part.

For me as a publisher, it's useful (though I certainly don't insist on it) to have my poets on Facebook, because I regularly post as HappenStance Press. My posts aren't personal: they're about new publications or publishing issues, and if these posts mention a particular poet, their name will be 'tagged'. That means such posts will automatically show up in that poet's 'feed', if the poet is on Facebook. And the poet's friends may also 'share' the post, which can be useful for publicity purposes. I also have a private Facebook group where HappenStance poets can communicate with each other, visible only to members of that group. But to participate in a secret group, you have to have a Facebook page to start with.

On my website, there's a bio page for each of the poets I publish. An interesting-sounding author may be as much of a 'hook' in terms of getting interest in the publication as the book jacket. Being a poet is not like being a novelist. A successful novelist may sell many thousands of books. A successful poet sells a few hundred. A successful novelist may receive thousands of letters a year – too many to reply to in person. A successful poet may get a dozen. The poets can certainly write back, if they feel moved to. Arguably, a 'successful' (sorry, this word is starting to ring hollow in my ears even as I write it) poet can't afford to ignore her or his readership because the number of English-speaking readers with a serious interest in contemporary poetry is so small. In 'What Next?', a *Guardian* article by Bloodaxe editor Neil Astley in 2008 (you'll find it online if you google it) poetry sales at that time were 0.06% of total UK book sales.

The internet offers a connection between poets and readers. It's a social medium. However, it's not like live conversation. It's riskier. If you go to a party or a reading, drink too much and say a number of daft things you later regret, the chances are nobody (including you) will remember them. But if you get over-excitable at home and post things you later regret on Twitter or Facebook etc., it's not so easy to make this disappear. Things said in print, on the web as on paper, have a permanence that's serious – because people 'share' them. The danger is that 'friends' on Facebook start to feel like actual friends. Some of them may be precisely that. But others are not. If you're new to these applications (or just a little careless), you may not be using privacy settings to divide 'friends' into different groups for different posts. (If I post family photographs, they're only visible to people I've tagged as Family. If I post Happen*Stance* publicity, the setting will be Public, and anybody can see it.)

I'm aware this can sound alarming. But if you assume *everything* you post or share is something you wouldn't mind appearing in a newspaper or magazine, you'll be fine. It's easy to observe Facebook thread interactions and either not join in at all, or only do so in a respectful and careful way.

Earlier in this book, I suggested that when your manuscript arrives on your prospective publisher's desk, she or he should already know your name and perhaps even have seen it popping up in a social network discussion. This could be advantageous if your contributions have been moderate and well-balanced. Perhaps you've shared links to interesting articles, or complimented other friends on new publications. But if your prospective publisher remembers you because you are the one who harangues publishers for favouring white, middle-aged, male poets, things may not go so well.

Often poets will use a Facebook page to share their triumphs and rejections. This can certainly contribute to the sense of fellowship, especially during periods of low confidence. But even here, it's sensible to think twice about what you post. If you announce you've had a poem accepted by *Poetry Review*, you'll get a string of congratulations. You'll also have a set of lurkers gritting their teeth because their poems have been rejected by *Poetry Review* for decades.

Rather than sharing your own poetry acceptances, how much better to have a friend spontaneously post a message on your page when the poem appears: 'Just seen your poem Buttering Parsnips in *Poetry Review* – and LOVED it!' This time some people reading the notification may go and track down your poem and read it. Or if they already have a copy of the magazine and didn't notice you were in it, they'll go and take another look.

Case Study

A friend phones in some agitation. She received an acknowledgement last year when she sent a full manuscript to a poetry publisher, but a year later, there has still been no yea or nay. So she has telephoned the publisher. He apologised: he has a backlog, he says, of over 1,000 manuscripts waiting to be considered. She should feel free to approach other publishers. What should she do?

It is a horrible situation. What *should* she do?

She should be aware that this publisher, despite his backlog, is continuing to publish several poetry book titles each year. These are likely to be books from poets he was familiar with long before they made an approach to him. He doesn't know her or her work.

When he finally gets to it, the chances he will accept are nearly as remote as winning the lottery. If she finds another publisher he will be mightily relieved.

She should start looking for another publisher, but do some careful preparation first.

Not an Ending

He never lived in that valley
or anywhere else. On the night in question
he did not stand by the river or ignore
the new rain or drop stones into the water.
There were no tree songs around him,
no unidentified birds, no flowing to the sea.

Her eyes were not blue. Those were not her boots.
She walked more quickly. He did not hear
her last word or want to. He may
have shrugged, but never shook.
He had no regrets and would not think
of her again. He would not think of her again.

Andrew Waterhouse, from *In*, Rialto Press 2000

R EAD ANDREW'S POEM, ONE OF the saddest of poems. Do you
notice the flat defiance of tone, the way the sentences, laid un-
apologetically one top of the next, are almost like a police statement
taken down from a witness?

Read it out loud to yourself so you feel the way the rhythm stresses
the negative words: *never, not, no, no, no.* There are key assertions at the
start of several lines: 'He never lived', 'he did not stand', 'There were no',
'Her eyes were not', 'He had no regrets'.

How very different it sounds when the poet concedes a variation 'He
may / have shrugged'.

With this in mind, write about an occasion when you didn't do
something or say something. Or someone else didn't do or say some-
thing.

Or do what this poem does: describe the *opposite* of what happened.

Your theme is regret. Two six-line stanzas.

When you've finished, if you've written in the third person (she/he)
change it to first (I), or vice versa.

Chapter Seven: Should poets blog?

'Perhaps people become publishers just to endlessly prolong a conversation on books.'

—Roberto Calasso, *The Art of the Publisher*, Penguin Books 2015, tr. Richard Dixon

SHOULD POETS EAT PEANUTS? Should they drive cars? Should they go on holiday to Finland? Of course they should – if they want to. And if they want to, they should write blogs.

But perhaps I should be putting this question in a different way. Should poets consider blogging as part of their strategic approach to getting their work published? That's a question worth addressing.

I mentioned earlier that it's useful, when your manuscript arrives on the publisher's desk, if they already know your name – in a positive context. So if you're a respected blogger, it could be helpful to you in many ways. But it's not something you should start lightly. It's like any other form of writing: only worth doing if you're going to do it well, and doing it well means time, commitment and self-discipline.

But first, what does it mean these days to 'blog'? Here's the first paragraph of the Wikipedia entry:

> 'A blog (a truncation of the expression weblog) is a discussion or informational site published on the World Wide Web consisting of discrete entries ('posts') typically displayed in reverse chronological order (the most recent appears first). Until 2009, blogs were usually the work of a single individual, occasionally of a small group, and often covered a single subject. More recently 'multi-author blogs' (MABs) have developed, with posts written by large numbers of authors and professionally edited.'

Which tells you, perhaps, how widely the definition now extends. Many major media outlets think blogging essential, because it increases the traffic to any website. If you think in a media-savvy way, what you want is attention. So anything that increases the 'hits' is valuable.

But if you think in a poet-way, what sort of attention do you want? There are poets who regularly post poems on their own blog pages (or even Facebook pages), and invite comments from their readers. This is understandable and harmless, unless that poet wants to send the same poems later to magazine editors or book publishers who want work that hasn't been previously published. If you put poems on your blog or your website, you're publishing them. It isn't the same as sharing them with friends, even though it may be mainly your friends who see them. The verb 'publish' traditionally means to prepare or produce a book or magazine for sale, but another meaning is 'to make a public announcement of' or 'to disseminate to the public'.

Disseminating to the public is precisely what a blog does. If you want to share poems in progress with friends on the web, there are plenty of un-public ways. You can set up a private Facebook group, for example. Or communicate with friends by email. Or use an online critiquing group like the Internet Writing Workshop.

But most poets don't blog, and those who *do* don't necessarily blog about poetry. Take a quick look at some of the UK's leading poets. The current laureate, for example, Carol Ann Duffy. Does she blog? Take a look at her Picador page. She is blogged *about*; she does not blog.

What about Gillian Clarke, currently National Poet of Wales? A visit to her website: www.gillianclarke.co.uk will confirm that she does not blog.

Okay, what about Scottish makar, Liz Lochhead? Check out her page on the Scottish Poetry Library website. Lots of information about Liz, but no mention of a blog.

Sinéad Morrissey, then, Belfast's first ever poet laureate? The poet does many things. Blogging is not one of them.

Perhaps they don't *need* to blog. And perhaps you don't need to either.

But you might want to, for a variety of reasons. There are poets who blog successfully (by 'successful' I mean poet-bloggers who have built a regular following). As I said, it's a serious commitment.

To blog, you need to know you can kick start good prose pieces on a regular basis. Not all poets write well in prose (their poetry's not necessarily the worse for that). Prose is a whole different ball game. You need to have something to say that people might want to read. Most of all you need dedicated time, because blogging well and regularly takes ages. This will be time you are *not* spending writing poems.

Take a look at some of the most effective poet-bloggers to see what can be achieved and what sort of commitment it takes. You might start with Anthony Wilson (anthonywilsonpoetry.com) whose blog at the time of writing is followed by 7,407 people. Anthony blogs about poetry, about cancer, about the conversations inside his head, about education (especially teaching poetry), currently about running – and a variety of other things. But mostly about poetry.

A couple of years ago, he began a series of blog entries called *Life-Saving Poems*, in which he picked a poem he loved each week, and wrote about it. Many people read the poems, commented and shared the link, which brought other readers. Public interest quickly expanded. In 2015, a set of 'Lifesaving Poems' from this blog were published as a Bloodaxe anthology, so the blog extended its reach to a paper readership. And Anthony is still blogging. He has a new series on poems and poets that deserve more attention, and he also invites guest bloggers. If you google 'Anthony Wilson' + 'What you read in 2015', you'll come to a list of the blog posts that attracted most readers. Several of these are by guest bloggers and several of those guests are poets.

If you take a look at the blog entry for 'Rogue Strands' (poet Matthew Stewart's blog) Tuesday December 1st 2015, he lists what he sees as the best UK poetry blogs of the year. From this list, which is a great place to start, you can see not all the poetry bloggers are poets but many are. These are poets who enjoy sharing their thoughts in prose, and often they have a particular angle. It might, for example, be their own 'poetic journey'. But equally it might be either a review blog or a reading diary. Or a set of opinions. Or a publisher's blog like my own, where sometimes I write about poetry, but more often about issues associated with publishing it.

It's easy to set up a blog site, or to have a blog added to your website (if you have a website). People do it all the time. In the first few months, you often find a series of spirited entries. Then the posts get fewer and fewer. There has to be an 'angle' or a spur to keep a blogger going, and to keep readers enjoying the experience. You could blog about each poem you had accepted by a magazine. But who would want to read it? More fun to blog about rejection, except you couldn't keep it up. That, too, would get boring after a while.

But there are other topics, that might win you a readership and teach you something at the same time.

- You could blog about poetry magazines and journals – maybe a different one each month. You could interview editors.
- You could blog about poetry websites.

- You could blog about dead poets.
- You could blog about poetry anthologies.
- You could blog about new poetry collections you found especially interesting.
- You could blog about arts events.
- You could blog about translated poetry.
- You could blog about spiders.
- Or recycling.
- Or cycling.
- Or travel.
- Or crime.
- Or arthritis.
- Or mental health.
- Or your husband.

(Maybe not the last. Or not without permission.)

Or you could go and write a poem instead.

Case Study

Twelve poems arrive from P.R. Runcible who would like me to consider his third collection *More Ways of Killing a Pig*. His first was from Peterloo in 2007, next from Badleg Books 2011. He says I reviewed the second one in *Ambit* and liked it so he wonders if I would consider his third.

Did I? I go and check. Right enough, I once wrote some warm things about his way of coming at ideas from odd angles in *Hurray for the Parsnip*. But why aren't Badleg Books bringing out the third? Maybe the last one didn't sell. Or maybe he fell out with the editor, my old friend Barney Gubbins.

So why has he chosen *me*? I only bring out two books a year at most, and anyway I need more women just now. Has he ever *read* any of my books?

The poems are quite fun though. I like the one about the curious pinkness of lettuce. I think I'll give Barney a ring to get the real story about this poet.

Influenza

The nearest we come again to the pure
passivity of a child is when ill
we lose all initiative and power,
and the animal body wells back up to fill
the vacancy left by a folding self.
The raw and swelling senses, reborn,
freed from will and action, return
to first impressions. Now the sun is felt

warm as gold, immanent in every room,
glorified even in the bathroom chintzes;
a solitary dog barks down the distances
of August fields; downstairs there is a low hum
of voices, the strength toward which we fall,
blissfully, as if towards something eternal.

Tom Duddy, from *The Years*, HappenStance 2014

DO YOU REMEMBER THAT feeling of being sick in bed as a child? The mixture of nightmare and comfort – especially the 'low hum of voices' from healthy adult people somewhere just out of reach, and the 'solitary dog' who 'barks down the distances'?

Think back to some experience of being ill, that time when you're alone and can just hear the world going on somewhere distant without you.

Put yourself mentally into that space and then write about it. What can you hear? Precisely what do your ears pick up?

Your poem is about sound and space.

Chapter Eight: Getting attention

'Let me have another opportunity of years before me and I will not die without being remember'd.'

—Keats to Fanny Brawne, March 1820

'WOULD YOU HAVE A look at these poems for me?'
The first time I encountered this question, I was moved. Of course I would look at the poems. I was a college teacher. Besides, didn't I write them myself? Didn't I understand? Many poems, many writing groups, many poetry competitions and magazines later, I know how much I did not understand about poetry and the matter of building a public readership.

It was 'Frank McBard' who asked the question, and Frank who began to clarify things. Frank is just one example – because the world has many Franks, young and old, male and female.

Frank was 'widely published' long before we met. Later, to his credit, he became aware that his early poetry 'successes' were exploitative scams, but this didn't hold him back.

He had a brief phrase of entering competitions and submitting to national and international magazines. However, he had little success and sensibly decided the returns weren't worth the outlay. Instead, he attended evening classes (mine among them) to build confidence. To learn. And learn he did. He learned what other poets were doing. They performed in pubs; some printed and sold copies of their work in the local library.

Frank had a better idea (this was before the internet, before computers in homes and libraries). He had sets of poems reproduced in small photocopied booklets and distributed them free. He selected local issues and people – wrote verses especially for them – presented them with these poems as gifts. He sent press releases about himself to the local paper, with photographs. Soon he was widely referred to as 'local poet Frank McBard'. This gave him a sense of satisfaction, although he aspired to more.

McBard's title as 'local poet' was fully deserved. Rarely does a person labour so hard and at such personal cost simply to earn the name of 'poet'. I have deliberately not commented on his actual poetry – because it is irrelevant. Frank's outstanding 'gift' was for getting attention.

And it mattered to him – mattered enormously – that he should be recognised as a poet.

As for the famous dead poets I grew up idolising – each of them had a touch of Frank; and if they did not, then they co-habited with a Frank substitute who did the work for them. Failing all else they were 'discovered' posthumously by an academic McBard who rode to fame on their coat-tails (the quality of determination is not restricted to poets).

The only difference between the great poets and Frank is that superior writing can be marketed in different places. William Wordsworth, Sylvia Plath, W.H.Davies, Christina Rossetti, Anna Wickham, Hugh Macdiarmid – these writers *slaved* for their place in the literary canon. They dedicated themselves to selling (metaphorically and, on occasion, literally) their work, sometimes to the detriment of much else in their lives. They combined writing talent with marketing gusto.

Would Frank have come to be locally 'known' without his self-marketing ability? I am certain he would not. Would he have become 'known' if he was a superb writer with no self-publicising determination? I fear – no. Success in the contemporary literary world can only be a reality for those who possess both talents, though not necessarily in equal proportion.

All this makes me wonder about those writers who don't attempt to publish their work. Where are they? Do they really exist? What has become of their work over the last millennium? And how many of them are women?

McBard, I am not ashamed to admit, inspired me. I saw his efforts and redoubled my own. I was richer than Frank and could buy more stamps and send to more magazines, buy more books, read more poetry, write better. I had the benefit of an academic education and a lifetime study of literature. And so it began. At first, my poems were summarily rejected by a number of outlets. Then the acceptances started. Like Frank, I wasn't easily satisfied. When you start to succeed, it fuels the need for such satisfaction to continue, though that need is not always met and, as you go along, your goals may change.

The highest honour for any poem is to be remembered and passed on, and for this to continue long after the name of the author is forgotten. The poet is not 'an important fellow' as Stevie Smith said. But the poem doesn't get remembered unless somebody – usually the poet – gets it out there. You can't aspire to be Anon unless somebody reads, or hears, your words.

I believe the craft – which is what I first cared about – succeeds or fails at home, where the poet is her or his own most demanding critic. The need for attention is another matter. Without it, there might be no published literature. Without it, the very best of our art would (and perhaps some of it does) end its life in a back cupboard.

Case Study

A poet writes in, enclosing an attractive bound edition of her poems. She tells me she has had many poems published in her local paper. They are very varied: some are funny, some are sad and some are about personal health issues. She has paid for 50 copies to be printed and bound 'to send to publishers like yourself'.

The book of poems has been self-published through a vanity press organisation, issued with an ISBN (international serial book number) and catalogued with the British Library. The job of publishing has been done. I look up the organisation she has used. It seems she paid at least £500.00 for the 50 copies of her book. She has done this in the mistaken belief that this is a good way to persuade an established publisher to print her work.

The poet doesn't know that submissions of poetry are normally on loose sheets of paper, and that the poet should have a magazine publication track record before approaching a publisher. No-one has explained to her that she isn't even writing the sort of poems that are in these kind of magazines.

Her best bet probably was self-publishing: she could have had three times as many copies printed for half the price and given them to her friends and family.

Write now: Riddles

'In thinking about creativity, one must be clear about the nature of success, disentangling it from the conventional associations of money and acclaim. [...] Success can never precede creativity as an aim; it can only follow as a result.'

—Alison Prince, in *The Necessary Goat & Other Essays*
on Formative Thinking, Taranis Books, 1992

DESCRIBING THINGS CLEARLY ISN'T easy. And sometimes you can describe them as clearly as you like and unless you tell the reader, they still don't know what it is you're describing.

Many poets write riddles unintentionally. They think the meaning is as plain as a pikestaff and unless someone actually asks them, 'What is this poem about?' (a question readers are often reluctant to pose), the poet may never know it's not self-evident.

But think about it – as soon as you use a metaphor, you're into riddle territory, and riddling is fun. It's one of the numerous tricks in the poetry player's repertoire.

Here are three riddles in Scots made by William Soutar, the Perth poet who died in 1943 after spending most of his adult life confined to bed. Hard to draw attention to yourself in these circumstances, but not impossible. Soutar was a reader: he devoured books, magazines and newspapers. He wrote to writers he admired. He developed literary contacts by correspondence. These turned into friends who visited and later championed his writing. He wrote for many kinds of readers, mostly adults but sometimes children. The riddles come somewhere between these audiences. I'll 'translate' them into English after their first versions.

1.

It has an ee but canna see:
It stands richt tipper-taed:
It can mak a man get up and run;
Yet we chain it wi a threed.

It has an eye but can't see:
It stands right tip-toed:
It can make a man get up and run
Yet we chain it with a thread.

2.

Its body is water; its banes is a breath;
And lichtly it walks on the wind:
But the hand that wud tak it maun aye be its death;
And the corpie be gey far to find.

> Its body is water; its bones are a breath
> And lightly it walks on the wind.
> The hand that would take it must kill it, and yet
> The corpse is a hard one to find.

3.

Wi a bairn it winna be:
Wi a wife it winna gree:
Wi a man it winna dee.

> With a baby, none to see
> With a woman, it won't agree
> With a man, it won't let be

I think the first two are fairly easy to guess. I found the third one harder. (Answers upside down at the end of this section.)

Anyway, here's your challenge. Choose anything that features prominently in your life: something you see every single day. Riddle it. You don't have to rhyme but it's fun if you do.

(The riddles are drawn from *Riddles in Scots* by William Soutar, The Moray Press 1937.)

Chapter Nine: Thinking like a publisher

'But judgement was the basic founding element for the existence of the publisher, that strange producer who needs no factory and can even reduce his administrative structure to a minimum. Yet he has always had one undeniable prerogative: to say yes or no to a manuscript and decide in what form to present it.'

—Roberto Calasso, *The Art of the Publisher*, Penguin Books 2015, tr. Richard Dixon

WHEN YOU APPROACH a publisher or editor and ask them to consider publishing your poems, what exactly is it you're asking? What can a publisher do that you can't do yourself? And what's the difference between a publisher and an editor?

In this chapter, I'm going to encourage you to think like a publisher. You may not enjoy it, but it may help you understand why – when your beautiful manuscript arrives on someone's desk – they don't necessarily leap at the chance of taking it on, no matter how good it is.

The first thing to acknowledge is that poetry publishers are unlikely to profit significantly from publishing your book, though there's more than one kind of profit. If we consider the money side of things first, some titles won't cover their costs because they won't sell enough copies. A publisher may be relying on public funding of one kind or another, and at any time such grants can be withdrawn or reduced. This means they have to like your poetry (or you) a great deal to award it part of a restricted budget. So the issue isn't whether you're a good poet – that's an essential prerequisite. It's whether they like the way you write. Or like *you* a lot. Ultimately, this is personal. And yes, publishers do sometimes publish their friends.

But there are different publishing models. Modern print techniques allow publishers to print books cheaply in small quantities, and this is precisely what they do. Some middle-range publishers issue contracts that ensure they won't lose out financially. They may stipulate that the author buy a certain number of copies in advance, or by a set date (a kind of reverse of the traditional publisher's advance against royalties, where *they* pay *you* in anticipation of expected sales). Authors feel understandably nervous about this, though it isn't 'vanity publishing' as such, since these publishers reject more poets than they accept.

The other form of profit is kudos, and this is also significant. The poetry editors of large publishers (which generate their main income from other genres) may be less concerned about sales than reputation. If your work is sufficiently distinctive to be shortlisted for an award or some other attention-catching status, the publisher gets kudos and sometimes this is worth as much if not more than money. Poetry is a kudos medium, like most literary forms. (I use the word 'literary' in this context as the opposite of 'popular'. Popular titles sell in quantity. Literary titles sell to a small reading public, sometimes regarded as an 'elite'.) When a publisher considers your work, he or she is likely to have both money and kudos in mind, as well as the balance between them.

Suppose someone *does* like your work enough to offer to publish, here's the process they commit to. A small publisher may take on all these roles; a bigger one will have its own poetry editor, and other staff will take on typesetting, production, publicity etc.

Hands-on editing:
- intense reading of your work and selection (often in discussion with you) of the best poems to go into the publication
- patient scrutiny of each poem to ensure it justifies its inclusion and it's working as well as it possibly can. This could involve pruning, revision of punctuation, line breaks or word choice (especially if there are repetitions or obscurities you haven't spotted)
- agreeing acknowledgements, accreditations, note of prior publications etc.

Type-setting:
- designing the form and appearance of the book
- putting the poems onto the pages
- designing the book jacket

General editing
- checking type-setting, sending proofs for you to check
- preparing the information or blurbs for publicity
- proof-reading: a good editor will proof-read your work or get someone else to double and triple check for accuracy and you should do the same

Publishing:
- registering your book's details, cover price and ISBN (international serial book number) which will make it purchasable through bookshops and online
- generating a bar code from the ISBN for the book jacket
- uploading electronic files (if the publisher is part of an electronic registration scheme or a Google search facility)
- drawing up a contract stipulating terms (these may include an advance payment. There may be a royalty agreement too i.e. a percentage from sales to go to you, or no payment at all – it depends how the publisher is operating and what sort of sales they anticipate. Your minimum expectation is a specified number of free copies of the book, and thereafter the ability to buy more at a reduced price. A reputable publisher bears all production costs.)
- working with a printer to set up the job, agree price, materials, dates and method—which could be a specified print run or a print-on-demand arrangement (If it's a print-run, the publisher decides how many to order. The more you print, the lower the unit cost but the higher the cost for the job. The risk lies in estimating how many are likely to sell. With new print-on-demand technologies, publishers can order as many or few as they like, and order more at any time because electronic masters are kept on file. POD books need never go 'out of print'.)
- paying the printer's bill
- arranging distribution for storing and despatching the goods
- supplying copyright libraries (by law the publisher must send a copy of each title to the British Library and then five more copies to the Agency for Copyright Libraries)

Publicity
- larger publishers will have publicists responsible for despatching review copies, entering titles for prizes, issuing press releases, sending complimentary copies to influential readers etc. (Smaller publishers will do some of this but may also expect the poet to take on some of this work.)

Sales
- the sales of larger publishers will be handled through the usual online websites, as well as some bookshops; smaller publishers may sell through their own web shops: they may also ask poets to approach local bookshops about stocking copies
- poets are usually offered copies of their own books at a discounted price so they can sell them at readings and events (some small publishers make most of their sales direct to the author)

Bear in mind that while engaged in this process on your book, your publisher/editor may also be:
- worrying about the books on last year's list that haven't sold
- considering balance in this year's list: are there more men than women? Is there ethnic diversity? etc.
- actively working on six other titles
- dealing with correspondence
- reviewing new submissions
- considering second, third, fourth collections by poets in their list, including *Selected, Collected, Complete* editions
- considering reprinting, revised editions, new editions
- going to meetings, events, festivals, funerals
- writing rejection letters
- answering phone calls
- writing articles, reviews, thank you letters, press releases
- supplying information to researchers, interviewers etc.
- taking care of mail order, posting and packets
- updating the website
- making funding applications
- making dinner
- visiting a therapist

Some publishers are even writing poems, bless them.

Soup

At the end of the month it's often swede but even this
with garlic, a small onion, perhaps a stick
of celery, maybe that carrot dried out in the fridge –
you could do worse. The garlic comes
from taking childhood taste,
growing it up, and learning.
A fresh-pulled bay leaf helps (and if there's time
ruffle the dead leaves underneath: breathe in).
The parsley on the windowsill, all stalk,
gives off its winter-watery smell.
The pepper cosies up.
Or when it's leeks
down to half-price, and potatoes left
from weekend baking, or sweet parsnips, there's
a thicker warmth to insulate the house
against hard times, rooted in winter, lasting
longer than you think.

D.A. Prince, from *Common Ground*, HappenStance 2015

FOOD CRITICS WRITE ABOUT food all the time, and it can be a sort of poetry in itself. But there's also the whole business of how taste and smell bring back memories – the aging parsley with its 'winter-watery smell'.

D.A. Prince's poem evokes comfort in basic ingredients, using leftovers, making things last. Even the poem is made of not much when you think about it: just the idea of making soup at the end of the working month when there's not much left to work with.

You can make a poem with very little. You only need the simplest ingredients. Here they are: you can have one carrot. If you don't have one to hand, you may have to acquire one or use another vegetable (though carrot is the best). You need at least half an hour to do this properly, as you'll see from the following 'recipe'.

This is a mindfulness exercise, so perhaps you know the routine already. Here's how it goes.

Approach the carrot with respect. This is not just any old carrot.

Lay it on a surface and look at it carefully, every little whisker and blemish. Then pick it up and feel the knobbly skin and texture.

Next peel it, if you like it peeled, and listen to the sound of the slicing skin and the rubbery little whistle as it lands on the plate or the whoosh as it goes into the bin.

Smell it. What does a carrot smell of? I can't remember. I'd have to go and do this to be sure. It smells orange, doesn't it?

Time to put a bit in your mouth. Don't crunch right away, just allow your tongue and mouth to feel its shape and angles. What does it taste of un-crunched? Now bite and savour. How does it sound? How does it feel? How does it taste?

Now write a poem titled 'Carrot'.

It may not be about carrots.

Chapter Ten: Making your approach

'A statement that the author's aunt thinks him a budding genius is not helpful, but the information that she could secure the adoption of the work as a text-book in several important schools or colleges could be.'

—Stanley Unwin, *The Truth About Publishing*, George Allen & Unwin Ltd, 1926

LET'S ASSUME YOU'VE IDENTIFIED a publisher to whom you want to make an approach. You've got a set of poems and you think they'll make a good book or pamphlet. You think there's something a bit different about them (more of this later in chapter 20), and you've done your homework on that publisher.

So what do you know about her?

- name: Liddy Morton-Solère
- name of imprint: *Prosody*
- she is very busy and has too much poetry already (of course)
- she publishes at least one first collection each year, and up to three
- she is half-French and was born in Paris
- one of her books was shortlisted for an award last year, and you've read it and (thank goodness) you like it
- she published a new book by Jasper Jumpy recently: Jasper lives quite near you and you went to the local launch in a bookshop and bought the book, though the publisher wasn't present (nice book, you liked it, especially after having heard its author read)
- she's just brought out an anthology of poems about food, in which you had a tiny poem about potted prawns
- she publishes a wide range of types of poetry, but mostly mainstream, which is what you probably are
- the debut poets she has published in the last five years were all under 30 (you are 52)
- she has published three collections of poetry of her own with another leading publisher (you have read two of these and found them hard going)
- she runs a house magazine called *Quirtles*; you like some of its contents – other bits mystify you completely

- her submission guidelines suggest 12 poems and a proposal
- she gets some public funding but the grant was halved last year

Okay, so here you go. You're going to send a dozen poems that will somehow catch Liddy Morton-Solère's attention and convince her to ask for more. How are you going to manage this?

There are ways *not* to do it, but it's hard to be absolutely prescriptive because publishers and editors are, as I said in chapter three, not all the same. They are radically different people. Let's begin with your covering letter, because it's almost certainly where Liddy Morton-Solère will start too. If you are courteous and professional, I think you won't go far wrong.

Select your facts carefully but be truthful. Do not over-egg this pudding. The publisher, if she likes your work, will be the one to praise it. Don't tell her in advance how brilliant it is – it will put her off.

Keep the letter succinct, not much more than one side of A4.

Don't attach a CV, listing publications since the year dot. When and if she wants this information, you can supply it. That time has not yet come.

Your letter will be typed, unless you have absolutely beautiful handwriting, in a size 12 font. It should highlight your main strengths and demonstrate an informed interest in the publisher's work.

If you're lucky, the publisher will have a dim memory of your name because of the potted prawns poem (though this was edited by someone else), but it will do no harm to remind her. Here goes:

Your address

31 January, 2016

Dear Liddy Morton-Solère

I am attaching a submission of twelve poems, as advised in the submission guidelines on your website. I hope you might consider these for a possible first collection, with the current working title: *Inhospitable*.

I read the recent interview with you in *Magma*, in which you say: 'too much poetry all the time, but I still value unsolicited submissions, especially from poets who read, as well as write, poetry'. I certainly do both, and I hope this set of poems may reflect that.

My proposed collection covers a range of styles and topics but one central theme is restaurants (I ran a restaurant in Paris for 15 years, and I know you have some connections there yourself). Many of the poems draw on voices of workers in the food industry and even, on occasion, the voices of the food they prepare ('Potted Prawns', was recently included in your own Battleground anthology *Food Prints*, and before that in *Quirtles*).

I have had poems published in a wide range of UK magazines, including (recently) *The Rialto* and *Poetry London*. I had a first pamphlet published (*Hard Neck* from Brass Kettle) in 2014. It received some good reviews and, to my delight, is now into its second printing.

I very much admire the work of your press, and you publish some of my favourite poets, including Maisie Punk, Orlando Havering and Jasper Jumpy. I went to Jasper's recent launch of *Mariner* in Southhampton. His reading was wonderful and the book is a terrific collection, both in its thematic focus and delightful presentation. What a great cover – with that amazing photo of the albatross, and how well it fits with the title poem!

I am a member of a Stanza reading group and Jasper's book will be on our agenda next month. I also read regularly at poetry events in and around Sussex, both on my own and as part of a performance group called 'The Leaven in the Lump' (we've just had an invitation to read at Ledbury next July).

Thank you for your time. I look forward to hearing from you.

Yours sincerely

[Whatever your name is, written by hand, and typed legibly below that as well.]

This letter takes account of some of the things a publisher has at the back of her or his mind before even approaching the poems. Remember the publisher is looking for reasons to say No. The publisher has already got more than enough poems.

From this letter the publisher can see that the poet

- has deliberately chosen them, not just picked them out of a hat;
- knows something about their list;
- has a decent magazine track record;
- has already built something of a readership;
- is active in reading and writing, with connections and friends who could help publicise and buy books;

- can express ideas coherently in a letter;
- has thought carefully about the submission and how it might make a book that's a bit different from the rest.

This doesn't mean the publisher will read the twelve poems and say 'Send me more', but at least she's interested enough to take a look. (The restaurant idea *does* sound different...)

The twelve poems will be professionally and consistently presented. That means typed or word processed in a plain font (nothing fancy) e.g. Times Roman, Garamond, Calibri etc. The size of the font will be about 12, so the poems will appear at much the same size as they would on the page of a book. They will normally be single (not double) spaced. The poet's name and contact details will be on each page, somewhere that doesn't look like it's part of the poem. There will be no copyright symbols creeping in anywhere. (You automatically own the copyright of your own work. If you assert it on the page, it will just look naff.)

Some publishers have more specific requirements about submission and will tell you what font to use and so on. It's your business to check that out on their websites. But if they don't say anything, the guidelines above will do nicely.

Case Study

A sheaf of poems in the post. Not a name I've heard of before and all prior publication seems to be in ezines. The covering letter invites me to read more about the poet by going to www.readallaboutme.com and I can also read a poem every day on her blog http://allaboutme_blogspot.com. Good grief – *every day*! No S.A.E. enclosed, just written note which reads: 'Do not return poems. Recycle manuscript. Email response to poet@readallaboutme.co.uk'

The poems go into the shredder as suggested by their author. No intention of visiting her website (no time). As for email, I reply by letter in S.A.E. or nothing. Yet another poet who ignores submission guidelines. A poet who doesn't use the net may have an excuse. A poet who invites me to visit her website should make sure she's looked at mine first.

Message to the Well-Meaning

It's not 'being positive'
that gets you through. No

it's something grittier – sharp, capable of hurt;
it would have you grabbing the very last crumb
from under your best friend's nose.
It's savage, stubborn, it's made of steel;
if you were in business the whole world
would hate your guts. So

the next person to come along and say
think positive and all that sort of crap
will get it right between the eyes.
For I'm a hard woman now.
I am diamond, carborundum,
and I wipe out fools.

Gill McEvoy, from *Uncertain Days*, HappenStance 2006

THINK ABOUT WORDS SAID in anger. Think about words that have been said in anger to you and by you.

Think about the most angry words you can remember. Perfectly horrible words.

Now write a poem that draws its strength from the way angry words were hurled out, or you wish they had been. Maybe they were never actually said.

Your poem must include at least one offensive word. By offensive, I mean a word you wouldn't use in formal company. A swear word. Or even two or three.

Chapter Eleven: Can you be a published poet and *not* do readings?

'It's true that many publishers' contracts now require authors to publicise. It's true that there are workshops on how to publicise your work and how to read in public and how to start a blog and it's true that many new(ish) – not, please, 'emerging' – writers feel some pressure to go along with this, but no, of course you don't have to. You can choose. You're a grown-up.'

—Charles Boyle, SonofaBook blog August 5, 2015

YOU MIGHT NOT BE able to do readings. You might not be able to speak. Or walk. You might be agoraphobic and unable to leave the house. You might hate the idea of 'performing' your work in front of other people. There are published poets who can't do readings or choose not to. Not many, but there's an exception to every rule.

The poet who doesn't participate in public events cannot check the box that says 'likely to sell because regularly participates in events'. So the publisher may know from the start this person is a bigger risk.

Does that mean they won't consider publishing the book?

It depends whether the poet can throw other key factors into the deal. One of these, of course, is writing brilliant poems. But since nobody can agree what 'brilliant' is (there are as many opinions as there are readers), this is a difficult one.

It may be that the *collection* is brilliant. This is not the same as writing brilliant poems, though you may think it is. Sometimes the whole is infinitely greater than the sum of the parts. The poet creates a book that will be remembered, rather than a book with a few poems that may or may not outlast their author.

It's likely in this case that the collection will be characterised by what I do not want to call 'an overarching theme' because I hate this horrible jargon, but *something*. A concept that pulls the poems together, or some respect in which the book clearly stands out from the rest.

Suppose you were unable to speak. Suppose you had had a stroke that had deprived you of the power of speech. Suppose these poems were your communication with the world. Perhaps your book title is *Power of Speech*. This strikes me as interesting, and assuming the contents were good, there's something here to interest a publisher, publicist and reader. So I wouldn't discount such a book as a possibility.

Let's take another scenario. You are physically able to read your poems aloud. There's nothing wrong with you except acute shyness. You do not *want* to read in public.

Your poems deal with the natural world. In fact, you've been researching the reproductive habits of the Highland Midge (*Culicoides impunctatus*) for the last twenty years. Insects are your world and they're in your poems – all over the place, nobody could miss them. These poems are full of violence and destruction: astonishingly disruptive imagery and lethal actions. The poems aren't pleasurable to read but once read, they are impossible to forget. The book seems to have something to say that's bigger than itself, perhaps about the human desire to self-destruct. It's titled *Impunctatus* and you've been working on it for over 15 years. Most of the poems have already been published in leading periodicals, and recently a group of three appeared in *Poetry Review*. Another, printed in the *Times Literary Supplement* last year just after the November 2015 terrorist attacks in Paris, led to some spirited correspondence in that paper about the extent to which humans and insects were like each other. So in a small way, you've acquired a name.

You approach a publisher with this collection. You don't mention your shyness. It doesn't occur to the publisher that someone who could write like this could possibly experience public reticence. The publisher thinks this book has every chance of winning the Forward Prize for Best First Collection, and makes you an offer.

Does it say in the contract that you must agree to appear at public events? It does not. Does the publisher assume you will appear at public events? Almost certainly, yes.

Will your failure to appear mean the book won't sell? No. The mould is always waiting to be broken. Don't put your photo on the back cover. Resist calls for publicity photos. Remember Greta Garbo, whose resistance to publicity drove MGM crazy, until finally they began to exploit the idea of the woman of mystery, silent, unsmiling and unfathomable.

There are at least two ways of bypassing the whole business:

1. You might secure acceptance from a maverick publisher whose choices are entirely dictated by personal liking, with no references to whether your book sells or not (but be aware that this may mean he or she won't promote it much either). This

could be a magnificently literary diehard, or someone rather different. Maybe you have a friend, for example, who publishes gardening books and would be delighted to include a poetry collection as a special addition – especially if gardening happens to be a central theme of many of your poems.

2. Instead of following all the careful preparation routes I've spoken of in previous chapters, you could focus simply on the collection competitions. There are many competitions for both pamphlet collections and whole books, though you may need to scrutinise the rules carefully to ensure they don't also trap you into a publicity spiral you can't or won't engage in.

The eligibility rules from the 2015 Anthony Hecht Prize, run by Waywiser Press, suggest that 'Entrants should not have published more than one full-length previous collection of poems, though they may have published an unlimited number of books belonging to other genres.' So far so good. But 'Entrants should be willing to read from their collections at the Folger Shakespeare Library in Washington, D.C., in autumn 2016, if they are chosen as the winner.'

So if you win, you're supposed to travel for several hours in an aeroplane to read your poems to an American audience in a library. However, you could cross that bridge when you come to it, as they say.

Let's take a look at The Poetry Business pamphlet competition. This year's competition, the thirtieth, 'invites entrants to submit a collection of 20-24 pages of poems for the chance to win publication by smith|doorstop, a share of £2,000 and other prizes.' At the first stage of selection, four winners are

> 'given the opportunity to submit a full-length manuscript to the second round of the competition, in which one of them can win book publication. The three first-stage winners will then receive pamphlet publication. All four winners will receive an equal share of the £2,000 prize money, and will have a launch reading organised by The Poetry Business and a selection of their poems published in *The North* magazine.'

Launch reading? Oh no! But when you look closely, you see the reading is only an *opportunity*. It could be an opportunity you declined.

Templar Poetry currently runs 'The Templar Portfolio Award' quarterly: four opportunities to submit groups of 10-12 poems, the prize being publication of a short poetry pamphlet and 20 free copies. They don't mind simultaneous submission. They have currently no requirement to participate in any public event for winners.

You could get a pamphlet or book into print this way, with the attendant publicity of winning a prestigious competition. You will have avoided making a planned approach to an individual publisher altogether. All you need is a collection that's a competition winner.

Case Study

Email titled 'Poetry Submittal'. Submittal? Interesting word. It comes through addressed to 'enquiries@flambardpress.co.uk' which means he's written to them and copied to several other publishers, of which I am only one. He requests my address, a contact name and contact number so he can send me some poems. This chap is emailing for information readily available on my website. He just hasn't looked.

Figuring he may be young, I send him a friendly email suggesting he's going about things the wrong way. I tell him about checking websites, following submission guidelines and the importance of track records, and explain that I don't take submissions by email. He writes back, thanking me warmly (clearly he still hasn't checked the guidelines) and pasting in one of his poems for me to see right now. Will I let him know what I think?

At this point, I make a mistake. I reply, reminding him I don't take poetry submissions by email but that in any case (as I said before) he would need a track record in the magazines before I would be interested. Besides, I say, the poem he has sent, with its long thin format, is not my cup of tea.

He replies again, sending me another poem with a different format because he's sure I'll like this one better. At this point I get sensible and submit to the inevitable. I don't reply.

Write now: Fear the worst

'THE WORST IS NOT / So long as we can say *This is the worst*', says Edgar in King Lear, and Gerard Manley Hopkins no doubt had that in mind when he opened one of his dark sonnets with the phrase 'No worst, there is none.' (This tremendous poet, who died in 1889, did not have a book of poems published until 1918, nearly thirty years after his death.)

So here's your topic. Perhaps the worst aspect of human experience never arrives, or at least not so long as you can look back at it and describe it. So write about the worst. The worst of anything you like. Doesn't have to be your life. Could be weather. Or a small cruelty. Or pain: the worst you ever had. Or someone else's worst, not your own.

My mother, who taught German, used to say, 'The Wurst is not so long as we can say: this is the Wurst', and *her* mother was wont to observe, 'There's an end to everything but two to sausages.' You see, thinking about the worst can take you unexpected places.

Here is the whole of Gerard Manley Hopkins' sonnet:

> No worst, there is none. Pitched past pitch of grief,
> More pangs will, schooled at forepangs, wilder wring.
> Comforter, where, where is your comforting?
> Mary, mother of us, where is your relief?
> My cries heave, herds-long; huddle in a main, a chief
> Woe, world-sorrow; on an age-old anvil wince and sing –
> Then lull, then leave off. Fury had shrieked 'No ling-
> ering! Let me be fell: force I must be brief'.
>
> O the mind, mind has mountains; cliffs of fall
> Frightful, sheer, no-man-fathomed. Hold them cheap
> May who ne'er hung there. Nor does long our small
> Durance deal with that steep or deep. Here! creep,
> Wretch, under a comfort serves in a whirlwind: all
> Life death does end and each day dies with sleep.

Chapter Twelve: How to write a book that wins all the prizes

'Publishers always lie.'

—Duncan Glen, poet and Akros Publications publisher, 2005

THIS WILL BE A short chapter. Why? Because I don't know how. Whatever the secret is, it only ever works once.

So, for example, Claudia Rankine won the Forward Prize for Best Collection in 2015 with *Citizen: An American Lyric*, a book of prose poems about racism published by Penguin. These are anecdotes and insights: short narratives and snapshots of real lives. Deliberately shocking, it shows what it's like to be black in twenty-first century America.

You can't do this twice.

Dan O'Brien's *War Reporter*, published by CB editions, won the Fenton Aldeburgh First Collection Prize in 2013 and was shortlisted for the Forward First Collection Prize. The book draws directly and continuously on correspondence between the poet and Pulitzer Prize winning war reporter Paul Watson.

You can't do this twice.

Alice Oswald's second book, *Dart* (2002), published by Faber and Faber, mixes verse and prose. It tells the story of the River Dart in Devon from a variety of perspectives. It won the T.S. Eliot prize in 2002.

You can't tell the story of a river twice.

But you *can* think about your USP. This is a marketing term and it stands for Unique Selling Point or Proposition. I don't want to brandish marketing language in the face of poetry, and I don't know what your USP is or may be, but I do know your poems are not like anyone else's.

A publisher or editor may help you identify what makes them distinctive, what holds the set together, or what – if you play around with content and style – could create a character for the whole book. But they may not. That's why you need to do it yourself. (For more about this, see chapter 20.)

Chapter Thirteen: Thinking outside the book

CONSIDER ALL YOUR OPTIONS – there are invariably more than you think. You'll need to do this because you *will* experience rejection. If you don't, you're either extraordinarily lucky or you need to be suspicious about your offer. You might start with this list, and select any that interest you.

- Self-publish through relatively new organisations like Lulu, Amazon's CreateSpace and Blurb who provide templates so you can set up your own pages, print as many or as few copies as you want, and make the book purchasable online.
- Self-publish through a good printer who offers an on-demand service for self-publishers. You'll find estimate request and price calculator software on websites of leading POD (print on demand) publishers as well as information about exactly how POD works (worth taking a look at cpibooks.com).
- Self-publish in a small volume with two or three other poets, who will share the cost and help promote—this will allow you to organise joint readings.
- Are you into performance? Take a look at poetry publisher Burning Eye Books ('never knowingly mainstream'), which has an additional service for performance poets who want to self-publish.
- Publish your work on an audio disc or downloadable electronic file—easy to make these now at home—especially good for a performance poet—sell via your website, or through social networking sites.
- Self-publish in Kindle format like Damilola Odelola with her debut pamphlet #000000.
- Enter competitions which offer pamphlet or book publication as prizes. (There are three issues here. 1. Are you hurling your entry fee down the toilet? 2. Have you any chance of winning? 3. Will they make a decent job of it?)
- Contact an agent (*Don't do this!* It doesn't work for poetry because people don't make enough money out of poetry for an agent to make money out of them.)

- Stay on the look-out for new poetry publishers. Send work to them as soon as they enter the fray (advantage: they are probably actively looking out for poets at this stage; disadvantage: you don't know what sort of job they will do).
- Go all out for pamphlet publication, rather than full-collection (it's hard to find a good pamphlet publisher, but not as hard as full collection. If your pamphlet's successful, it will improve your chances of book acceptance. You can get a list of UK pamphlet publishers free from the HappenStance website or www.sphinxreview.co.uk).
- Set up a writer's co-operative with some of your friends. If you have the right skills between you, you could establish your own imprint, buy a set of ISB numbers and publish each other's work
- Consider other print formats: publishing postcards of your poems, for example. You can make some beautiful things at Moo.com, and honestly it's not difficult.
- Create hand-sewn booklets, printed at home. These can be uniquely lovely. Sell at craft fairs, book fairs etc.
- Publish or self-publish by subscription. This sounds mysterious but isn't. You find sufficient people who agree to pay for a copy of your book in advance; this funds the cost of publishing. Often the names of the subscribers are printed at the back of the book. This works for a poet with a wide readership and a willing publisher. (Sometimes well-known, established poets publish by subscription.)
- Try crowd-funding to support your publication. This is the online version of subscription, and may work if your online networks are large and loyal. It's unlikely to work for you, unless your book has a USP that is both engaging and worth supporting. Crowd-funding offers something in return, if the requisite sum is raised – perhaps a signed copy of the book.
- Work with another artist, someone who uses a different medium – a painter perhaps, or photographer, or musician. Consider an exhibition, something that draws public attention and gets your name known.

- Forget book-length collections altogether. Stick to magazine outlets or local newspapers/radio etc. You do not HAVE to publish a book. Perhaps for you it's all about the poem, not the collection. And why not?
- Set up your own publishing house and publish other poets. Start with pamphlets. You'll learn a huge amount this way, and it won't do your own prospects any harm.
- Defer the whole idea for the moment. Start a poetry magazine or a writers' group instead. This will teach you, among other things, to see your own work more objectively.
- Attract attention to yourself by some highly original fundraiser: maybe performing poems by heart at every railway station in the UK and uploading videos to YouTube.
- Start a 'school' or 'movement' with a group of poet friends. Create a name for yourselves (The Middenists? The Quiddites?) Publish a group anthology. Get noticed.
- Put your current collection in a bank vault or in a box in the roof. Vow not to look at it for five years. Start next book.
- Postpone the issue of publishing for two years. In that time, do as much poetry reviewing as you can – the best possible way to learn about what is getting published, and by whom.
- Are you reasonably affluent? You may not want to pay for your book to be produced. It can feel like a cop-out. But you could pay for a mentor to give you some useful advice. Many established poets offer such a service.
- Or you could invest some money in supporting an event at an arts festival. If you offer enough money to pay a poet or two, plus their accommodation and expenses, you could become a formal sponsor. It's a great way to meet people, create warmth and feed into a system that you hope might one day feed you.
- Apply to study for an MA or MLitt. Get some quality constructive criticism for your work and your future planning. Meet other writers with shared concerns.
- Start working on connections. Get out there and meet people. You know all about 'no unsolicited submissions'. So get yourself solicited.

What you choose to do depends on your strategy (if you have one), and your strategy is affected by a number of factors, not all of which are within your control. If you're 22, for example, you have time on your side. You can think in the long-term, and you're a good proposition for a publisher who's mainly printing aging poets, a couple of whom die off every now and again. If you've developed a set of strong poems and you're under 30, you can apply for an Eric Gregory Award.

If you're 62 or 72 (or 82 or 92) it's more difficult. You may feel you have a closer acquaintance with time's wingèd chariot than you care to mention. You're too old for a Gregory and you can't read the small print on funding applications. On bad days it could seem that publication (if it ever happens) will be posthumous. When you get a reply telling you they liked your work 'but not quite enough', you may have a strong desire to tear all your poems into small shreds. But don't do that. You didn't write them just to tear them up. Why did you write them?

Sorry. That was a horrible question. I don't know why I write poems, and I don't know why other poets write them either, only that it's a life-enhancing necessity, a magical thing to do. Most poets write poems because they can't *not* write them. In other words, if you're a poet, you're not writing poems in order to get them published. But you would probably like someone to read them. You would like your ideal reader to read them. Where is that reader?

For some people, it might be enough if even *one* of their poems found the right reader. On the other hand, perhaps the highest accolade of all is to become Anon. A few of your words are remembered by millions of people. Your name disappears.

But look – none of that will happen unless you give it a kick in the right direction. It's no use just sitting around waiting for your poems to get spotted. Nothing will happen that way – there are too many competitors clamouring to be heard.

Resignation (ii)

And for the three months they make me stay
I refuse to add up insurance claims or carry a bell
walking the corridors wailing *leprosy, leprosy.*

I exist in geological time,
read War and Peace, eat biscuits.
My volcanic core becomes common quartz.

Pack ice crushes a stranded tanker:
its crude flood shines in rainbows,
drowns seals and gulls till the stink is Biblical.

Snow makes sound a muffled thing
and, as colleagues hurry to urgent meetings,
I choose a deep drift, unwrap my new spade.

I'm surprised how quickly
the space becomes large enough to enclose me.
How warm it seems.

Blocking the entrance, I leave a narrow gap
for air, less than a hand's span,
as little as I dare.

My breath forms crystals:
a smooth glaze across the roof and walls,
overlaying the striations of my digging.

No-one comes to find me
and when I sing to stay awake,
the icy layer builds up faster.

Sue Butler, from *Arson*, HappenStance 2011

72

THERE ARE MANY WAYS OF going into hiding. In her poem 'Resignation (ii)', Sue Butler uses the metaphor of digging a hole in the snow, a hole that's both comforting and claustrophobic.

Think about the idea of being hidden. Perhaps you recall a time when you literally went into hiding. Or maybe you remember hiding as a child. Or maybe you feel you're metaphorically hiding from something or someone right now.

1. Take yourself into a hiding place. Describe what it's like there. One stanza. Not more than ten lines.

2. Now put yourself into the position of a person hunting for you. What can they see? How do they feel? Not more than ten lines.

3. Put the two together. That's your poem.

Nobody has been found.

Chapter Fourteen: Game change & self-promotion

'But though I am bound to admit that there are far too many worthless books published, the real problem is not over-production, but under-consumption, or, to be more precise, insufficient sales. Most people have not yet learned to regard books as a necessity. They will beg them, they will borrow them, they will do everything, in fact, but buy them.'

—Stanley Unwin, *The Truth About Publishing*, George Allen & Unwin Ltd, 1926

I KNOW REJECTION IS problematic. It's no fun to have your work knocked back, even when it's done nicely. Nevertheless, rejection is likely to come your way at some point, regardless of the quality of your poems. If you don't match the expectations of your intended publisher, that probability becomes a certainty. *This is not personal.*

You already know that if you're approaching big-name publishers: Faber, Carcanet, Bloodaxe, Cape, Chatto, Picador, you must

- have an indisputably strong track record (that means you've placed a good number of poems in top magazines in the recent past)
- be familiar with the publisher's list and well-read in contemporary poetry (and this will be obvious from your approach letter)
- offer a book that's both arrestingly distinctive and marketable (not just another collection of good poems)
- have work that can both *fit* into the publisher's list (which in every case is 'literary', not 'popular') and *enhance* it with something new

In addition, you may

- already have published a successful pamphlet or other minor publication, which has attracted some attention and done well in sales
- have some accolade or other as a feather in your cap, e.g. Gregory Award, Aldeburgh 8 participant, trainee editor for the *Rialto* etc.
- have a reputation in some other form of writing or public life

To be attractive to these poetry giants, you're likely to be what Chris Hamilton-Emery calls a 'key player' in contemporary writing. What could this mean? You might, say, review for a quality arts publication, run a regular poetry event, tutor in Literature or Creative Writing, edit a reputable magazine or ezine, or something along these lines. They will think your writing distinctive enough and strong enough to have at least an outside chance of being shortlisted for a poetry prize. They will probably think you have a future too – a good prospect of producing more saleable books in the years ahead.

Why do they want all this? It's back to the two possible returns: cash and kudos. And on top of all of the above, the poetry editor will need to like the work. Which they may not. Over some things the poet has some control; others (including personal taste) are a matter of chance.

Let's assume you have *already* sent your collection to one, or more than one, of the 'big five' and it has come back as not wanted on voyage. Rejection. What's your next step?

You have various options. One of these is Rage. You could stomp around for a bit and do some teeth-gnashing.

What's going through your head? You could be wondering whether this is some kind of closed club with secret conditions for entry. You could be brooding about *quality*, which is what they all say they want. They're always banging on about *quality*. Every single book they publish is the best thing since sliced bread, if the back cover is to be believed. So why are some of their books full of instantly forgettable poems?

As they say of relationship status on Facebook, it's complicated.

Let's focus, just for a few minutes, on the issue of the 'quality of the work'. I dare suggest this: if your poems are fabulous, some of those top magazines *will* accept them gladly.

You've sent some already? They came back? Ah yes. This happens to all of us. And no, it doesn't mean your poems are weak. But they are either not strong *enough*, not to the editor's taste, or you've misjudged your market. You may believe you're writing in a literary way for a literary outlet, but you're not. You're either behind the times, ahead of the times, or writing in a different genre from the one required.

To test this out, you've got at least half a dozen top magazines to try, and if all of them say no, it's time for cool, honest self-appraisal. Your work may be fine, but not outstanding. There are worse things. And it doesn't mean it won't get better. Or that you don't have some poems that wouldn't, in due course, be accepted. Or the world may simply not yet be ready for your form of uniqueness. Did *Poetry Review* print Ivor Cutler?

Whatever the situation, if the top magazines don't like what you're doing, it's a good bet the top publishers won't either.

So what? Change your game plan, which was probably wrong in the first place. Take a look at middle-range publishers. How do *they* think? For the middle-range you have a better chance, provided you can find a publisher you like whose terms are agreeable to you.

Yet again, some have much higher reputations than others. I'm not going to tell you which, or why, because I don't want to be in court in a few months answering a defamation suit. You can find out, it's not hard. Keep your eyes open. Ask around. Talk to people with books in print.

Not only are there varying levels of reputation, there are many different ways of working in the middle ground. If you look at Jan Fortune's Cinnamon Press, for example, you'll see your best bet is to enter a competition – perhaps the debut collection competition. The competitions involve an entry fee. The entry fees are what keep the whole thing financially viable. The competition leads to a long list, a short list and finally publication for one lucky winner.

But Cinnamon publishes other debut collections too, and some of these authors are drawn from the mentoring scheme. This is where – if you've done your homework – you'll know how you get onto that Cinnamon mentoring scheme.

What is mentoring? Usually it means working with an established poet, who can guide you in terms of strengthening your work and your track record of publication, and perhaps help you build a readership too. For a while, you'll have an adviser who knows the ropes and can help you with a few shortcuts.

To be accepted on the Cinnamon mentoring scheme, often you'll be a person who has done well in Cinnamon competitions (which is where your entry comes full circle). You may well have had poems in Cinnamon's house magazine, *Envoi*. (There is more detail on the website and if interested in this publisher, you should take a careful look.) The mentoring scheme lasts a year and is described as 'intense'. Cinnamon reserves at least two publication slots at the end of the year for mentees / students.

Other publishers work, and think, in different ways. How about Worple Press, run by Peter and Amanda Carpenter? This imprint produces only a handful of books each year and these may or may not include a first collection. The website, at the time of writing, tells you no submissions are being considered until the end of July 2016. They welcome unsolicited work (they tell you what and how to send it) but remind you to 'consult the Worple backlist for a feel of what we are likely to consider worth publishing'. Poets 'who read or study contemporary poetry are more likely to be successful'.

How would you put yourself in the best position to interest Worple? Well, you'd have to read some of their books, and like them. You might even be able to review one of them somewhere, provided reviewing is something you do. This could mean the publishers would be familiar with your name when your manuscript arrived.

But maybe you know one of the poets on the Worple list personally? If you've been doing the hackwork of making contacts, creating a network of poets and friends, this is a distinct possibility. I'm not suggesting you wangle an introduction through one of their poets (this would be just as likely to put the publishers off) but such a person could give you a useful insight into the way things work at Worple. But at best this is going to be a long shot because the press prints so few books each year, and some are second or third collections from poets with whom they already have a relationship.

Let's take one more publisher who offers a different pattern again. According to its website, Indigo Dreams publishes 35-40 full collections each year, about three per month. This is a lot of books, and many of them are debuts, but it doesn't mean they'll leap at the chance of publishing your work. Indigo Dreams has been a limited company since 2010 and works to a fully commercial model (not all independent publishers do). They don't print books that make no money. (They do, however, run an annual competition with a prize of book publication for two winners every year.)

To approach Indigo Dreams about publication, you fill out a Publishing Enquiry Form. It's instructive to read this. Immediately you see what they want to know, you can begin to pick up on the thinking. One of the questions is 'Why do you feel Indigo Dreams Publishing is the right publisher for you?' If you want to send poems, you'll have to provide an answer that can convince both them and yourself. This, in fact, is true for any publisher.

But Indigo Dreams also has caveats on the enquiry form and website about the necessity for authors to be involved in promoting sales:

> 'The majority of poetry sales come from the poet's own readings and contacts. Trade sales are generally insignificant compared to Mail Order and author sales. You MUST be prepared to promote your collection to achieve maximum sales. It is unlikely we will consider a collection unless a level of success has been achieved in the poetry presses. If you genuinely believe you have a collection that is worthy of publication, and are willing to promote to achieve a good level of sales, then we would like to hear from you.'

You may be shifting uneasily in your seat, especially if you've always assumed the business of marketing and sales belongs to the publisher. But these statements do not mean the whole operation is a scheme to get money out of you. It means Indigo Dreams isn't prepared to lose money on its books and sees its authors as key purveyors of goods.

In fact, with small presses this is not all that unusual They don't have dedicated marketing departments. They don't have best-seller novels to bail them out when the poetry loses money. They may well think promotion is your job.

If you don't think promotion is something you should take the lead in, rule this publisher out. However, you'll find other presses too will regard promotion as – at the very least – a joint responsibility between poet and publisher. There is not a ready demand for single author poetry collections, and this is a fact. Even at the early stage, a publisher will be hoping a poet has given some thought to the matter of promoting the book.

Publishers have to think about sales. Sales happen if the poet has a readership. Sales happen if the book has something about it that will catch attention. Sales happen if the poet is already well-known in another field. Sales happen if the poet thrives on self-promotion.

Just occasionally, a publisher will take a big risk on a book. They believe it is *so* good they're going to print it whether or not anybody else likes it. In such a case, they are playing for kudos, if not now, then at some time in the future (and publishers *do* think about posterity with temerity). But this will be rare. It is not something you can expect to happen.

So part of your planning (I apologise if this fills you with dread) includes your plan for promoting the book after publication. You owe it to yourself and to your publisher. This may be something for which you have neither skill nor aptitude. But you may have a good friend who does, and who will help you. It doesn't have to be like ITV's *Stars In Your Eyes*.

All of this brings me to another inevitable consideration: how to create a readership for your work. And I don't mean your Aunty Susan and your six cousins in Fife.

Case Study

A set of poems comes in with a very interesting covering letter. The author has a background in theatre and performance, with good connections across the UK. This is a sequence titled *Refuge*, and it 'foregrounds the voices of individuals desperately looking for safety, many of them refugees of one kind or another.'

So far so good. Topical. Different. Attention-catching title. The author plans to create a performance based on these poems, involving herself and an actor friend: together they 'will take the event on a tour of 12 community centres' where they already have connections. What they need is a publication to take with them.

I love the idea. This is great. I start to read the poems.

Oh hell. This is just not my cup of tea. Love the idea. Do not love the work.

Downstairs

You visit friends and spend the night
and sleep late next morning and wake hearing
one of them on the phone downstairs,
you can't make out the words –

'She stemby demby frambers noyly from odgely nells,
but – flem the hurb? The gobbin. Yeah.
Sharmy gobbin hurb a harb the ubbage, gobbin gibbs!
Oh, yeah. And Billy Bebble donner whinny clong
the damey dominoes. Okay . . . Me too.'

— The words are not for you but in the cadences
and in the tonal modulations you hear
the infinity of human complication complicating itself
                                                    further
humanly beyond your little puddle of waking.
It's like an ocean, it's like a train,
it's like a train made of fulminous salty water
roaring softly down the track, downstairs and far away,

and soon as you wash your face
you see someone destined always to have missed
the train, the point, a soul without a ticket
walking always in the station when the human epic
has rolled away, bound for odgely nells,
bound for cities where the gobbin will noyly hurb the harb
and Billy Beb may clong the damey doms.

Mark Halliday, from *No Panic Here*, HappenStance 2009

P OETS INVENT PEOPLE, SITUATIONS and sometimes even words. In Mark Halliday's poem, the invented words are to do with mishearing or half-hearing real ones – though it's hard to imagine any real words that could resemble 'odgely nells'!

So here's your task. Write a poem about a person who is looking for something – perhaps a purse or a comb or a credit card. But invent a word for the thing in question. So the credit card might become a parmentium. A comb might be a flip-thingle. A purse might be a huspicle.

Put your invented word into the poem in place of the real one. If you like this idea, do the same with one or two other words in the poem. So the person in the poem is searching for something and the reader is searching for the meaning – because that's what all readers do in poems.

This doesn't have to be funny. It can be sad. People do lose words periodically, and are forced to create new ones or use tried and tested stand-ins like thingummy-jig, whats-it or hoojy-cum-piffery.

Chapter Fifteen: Relationships

'A good publisher is one who publishes one tenth of the books that he would like to, and perhaps ought to, publish. The religious and mythological works in the Adelphi catalog should therefore be seen as indicating a path along which actual books are accompanied in every direction by many virtual books, like friendly shadows. And I would like to add that a good publisher is also someone in whose books these friendly shadows are naturally and irresistibly brought to life.'

—Roberto Calasso, The Art of the Publisher, Penguin Books 2015, tr. Richard Dixon

TIME FOR A WORD about relationships. Poetry World is small. If you fall out with another poet publicly and bitterly, it creates a marvellous piece of gossip, which spreads fast. If you plagiarise someone else's poem, the news spreads even faster. People enjoy bad behaviour – so long as they don't have to invite it to dinner.

I suggest you try to be consistently and doggedly nice to poetry people. Perhaps you think you already do that, but think again. Don't tell me you've never browsed through a magazine that has rejected your poems, thinking 'so *this* is the drivel they preferred to me!'

Instead of letting rejection colour your feelings, focus on finding poems to like in magazines or ezines. You can find some: I know you can. (You don't have to like them all: only the editor ever does that.) When you find a poem you love, write to the author and say so. Be authentic. Only write when and if you really mean it. Try reading the online magazine *Snakeskin* which has a button under each poem for sending a response to its author by email. I have made several friends this way.

So an editor has rejected your poems without comment for the fifth time? Instead of sticking pins in a small doll, write a brief but charming letter about some review or article or poet in their last issue that you found interesting (unless there was nothing at all you liked, in which case cancel your subscription). By all means send the editor more poems, but not for a year. With luck, they may remember you warmly as a supporter of the magazine.

A publisher rejects your book with a cursory note, while accepting one by your friend. Don't blog about this experience sarcastically. Write and thank them for their time, and say how pleased you are about the news of your friend's book. Be remembered for being *nice*.

You think of yourself as the rejected creative. But a magazine editor makes a magazine with as much commitment, joy and despair as you make your poem. He or she desperately wants people to like it. Rejecting people's poems isn't fun: it's the downside of the job. Most of all an editor wants to believe he or she has made a publication that's worth something, that readers will enjoy. Each editor wants validation. If he or she deserves it, give it!

Publishers work hard to make a poetry list that readers will like. This is their baby. They dedicate most of their life to it. They don't enjoy rejecting poets. What they enjoy is finding they've made a set of books that readers can praise. If they deserve it, praise them.

I remember talking to a well-known magazine editor once about a particular poet who had sent many poems to their magazine but never had one accepted. I had chosen one of this poet's poems to print on a card, but had also taken to them as a person – we had had a delightful correspondence. To my surprise, the editor in question knew precisely who this person was, and also told me he liked their poems. 'Liked them?' I said. 'But you never accepted any!' 'No, not yet,' said the editor. 'But I would *like* to have done.'

If you support the arts, then support poetry – by taking an interest, buying publications when you can and responding intelligently to printed work. All these things make you a person worth knowing, a person whose work an editor would *like* to be able to accept, even if he or she doesn't. I don't suggest you do this as a method of deep and devious manipulation. I suggest you do it because nothing makes people more bitter than feeling excluded and rejected. But if you turn this around and make it your practice to support a group of poets and publications in which you're interested, it's a matter of whom *you* accept, whom *you* support, not the other way around.

What goes around, comes around.

All day, Hope sat alone beside the tree,
her head drooping, refusing to eat.

The new blue-ray widescreen TV arrived.
We were shown how to use the remote.

Just after Countdown she shuddered and went.
The news blared. No more lift-offs

from Cape Kennedy,
no more screaks for sunflower seeds.

The other chickens went oddly silent
as did we.

Diana Gittins, from *Bork!*, HappenStance 2013

HOPE, IN DIANA GITTINS' poem above, is the name of a hen, and this poem is about the day she died and all the ordinary things that were happening. But the small death mattered. It made a huge difference.

One of the many functions of poetry is to save memories from getting lost. Stuff happens in our lives and if we don't write it down, some things might escape forever. Families and old friends tend to keep memories alive. They get together at weddings and funerals and there are conversations that start, 'Remember the time when...?'

Write a poem that captures one of these stories. A true story about you or someone you know or once knew. It could be a story someone else told you.

Start your poem 'Remember the time when' because that will shift you into a conversational tone. But when the poem is finished, cut that opening phrase.

Chapter Sixteen: Creating a readership

'A poem is a potent thing. It has no natural place or purpose. It could be a spell, a song, a story, a sculpture, a treasure, a trinket, a toy, a riddle, a nugget, a potion, a record, a rune. A poem is a broken-off sliver. A poem is slippery.'

—One of three belief statements on Sidekick Books' website,
Jon Stone and Kirsten Irving

IF YOUR RELATIONSHIPS ARE working, you'll find creating a readership is already under way. If you're genuinely interested in the work of other poets, poetry editors and publishers, some of them will be interested in you. They will want to read you.

But first invest in reading and listening to *them*. There are poets afraid to read too much contemporary work because it might influence them. Be influenced. You're under the affluence of influence already. You're influenced by what you call 'poetry' and like, and what you call 'chopped-up prose' and don't like. You're influenced by advertising jingles and nursery rhymes, by the rhythms of news reportage and soaps. Whatever you write comes out the way it does because of other people's speaking and writing. Welcome to the human race. The influences were there before you even started running.

If you can't get to events (you live too far away, you're a wheelchair user and there's no access, you have no transport, there's a snowstorm, you are detained at Her Majesty's Pleasure), support what's happening in poetry in other ways. The World Wide Web provides YouTube performances, Vimeo, SoundCloud, recordings of public events, and sometimes live streaming too. Take a look. 'Follow' people. Observe sound poets, the avant garde, the old guard, the middle ground, the unlabelled-but-radical-ground.

If you can't get onto the internet, subscribe to magazines. Read the small print. Read the bio. Take notes. Read books. Buy books. Borrow books. Write to poets. Ask them questions. Do what you can. Bit by bit, find out where and how you can demonstrate an active interest, and do that thing. From small acorns mighty oak trees grow.

If you don't know where to start, sign up for the newsletter of the Poetry Library at the Southbank Centre. The Scottish Poetry Library also has one. Sign up for everything you can get, especially if it's free, and start weeding things out later.

Like it or lump it, if you're in this game, you have a relationship with what's going on. You're part of the interaction between readers and text, writers and text, readers and writers, publishers/editors and writers. You are part of the readership yourself, and ultimately you want that readership to notice what you write.

Of course, having your future book published is not the same thing as finding readers. (All it means is the book has found a *handful of* appreciative readers – the publisher/editor and, with a bit of luck, the publisher/editor's friends, all four of them.)

Your future book has to find its way to many more readers than that. How is this going to happen? These days both poets and publishers work feverishly at the business of promoting books and courting attention, and many of the books they produce still languish unsold. So if you want the business of publishing to be viable, you need to build that readership long before you send a publisher a manuscript.

If hardly anyone knows you even *write* poems and your work hasn't appeared in a wide range of magazines already, it's not looking good for your publisher, which usually means it's not looking good for you. On the other hand, if you're extremely well-known in another sphere – if you're a TV presenter, a politician or serial killer – your book may sell remarkably well because the whole business of publication will make a 'good story'.

Or if you can find a maverick publisher who will spot you as a truly wonderful exception to the rule, a person worth losing money on – then you could be in with a chance. But mavericks are thin on the ground.

Think long and hard. Where *are* poems widely read? Can you get your poems into that place? It's possible, for example, that you regularly dip into an anthology, such as Bloodaxe Books' *Staying Alive: Real Poems for Unreal Times* which at the time of writing has no fewer than 65 reviews on Amazon. (Yes, there *are* books of poetry that sell well and are widely read. They are not single-author collections like yours is going to be.)

How do you get into popular anthologies? People shortlisted for poetry competitions often find their poems included in a competition anthology, but this doesn't mean the resulting anthology will be widely read. There are anthologies and anthologies.

The Forward Arts Foundation every year produces an anthology that claims to be 'an annual anthology of the best of the year's poetry'.

How do you get into that? Usually, it's selected by the Forward Prize competition judges from books printed that year, one of which you don't have (yet). But they also select from individual poems entered in the 'Best Single Poem' category. How do you get your poem entered for 'Best Single Poem'? A magazine editor will enter it. They will pick it out from all the poems they published that year and nominate it for 'best'. How likely is this to happen? Well, your poem has to be in the magazine before it's a possibility.

But there are other anthologies. The Emma Press, one of the newer poetry imprints, is producing anthologies that are eye-catching and promise well. The *Emma Press Anthology of Mildly Erotic Verse*, for example, is something even a casual browser might pick up. And The Emma Press invites submissions. So what do you do? Go to the website. Read everything you can about the press. Sign up for the newsletter. Buy a couple of recent publications to see what they're like – maybe one of the previous anthologies. Read the submission guidelines and then send a poem, if you have one that fits the bill.

Or take a look at Valley Press (another relatively new publisher) which at the time of writing is inviting submissions of poems connected with the county of Yorkshire. And so on. There are always new things happening.

If you win the National Poetry Competition, your poem may also be of interest to anthologists, because it will certainly attract a lot of attention. Even getting the second or third prize is worth a bob or two. First you have to win that competition. I don't know what makes a competition winning poem, but I do know most poems don't have it.

Many aspiring poets concentrate mainly on competitions and forget the magazines. To my mind, when it comes to building a readership magazines are more important because poets and editors read them. But maybe you don't have time to wait six months for a magazine editor's response. Maybe you're already in your eighties. Or maybe you have reason to suppose you won't be around at all in a year's time.

How can you build a modest readership fast? The answer is in your network of contacts and friends. Who reads poetry? Who buys poetry? Mainly poets. So you need to know lots of them. You need to be exchanging poems with poetry friends. Some of your poetry friends will go to events with open mic opportunities. This means anybody can volunteer to go up and read a poem. You're too shy? Never mind: get your friend to read yours. Or read in disguise. Start putting your work out there! If you regularly do open mic – and there are now events all over the country featuring such things – you will become confident about reading in public. You may even enjoy it. You'll learn what works for a live audience, and what doesn't. It's an important and obvious way of building a readership, though I am aware it isn't possible for everybody to do this. You're a poet. You're creative. You can think of other ways too.

A case in point was M.A. Griffiths, who did not attend poetry events physically but began to participate in Poetry World online in 2001. She never pursued publication through traditional channels; her prime motivation was the joy of making poems as well as she could. But she relished interaction with fellow poets on various Internet forums, including Sonnet Central, where she volunteered as a moderator. On the rare occasions she submitted work for publication, it was to ezines, where links to pages could be shared with online friends. She used the pseudonyms 'Maz' or 'Grasshopper'. I 'met' her as Grasshopper during the years when she edited *Worm*, a monthly poetry magazine distributed by email, to which I contributed more than once.

Grasshopper died unexpectedly and prematurely in 2009. Her online poetry friends were shocked and saddened. They began collecting her poems with the intention of making a book of them. Roger Collett of Arrowhead Press had noticed her work online long before she died and had suggested she send him a submission. She never took up this offer. But now he offered to publish a posthumous book, and after much preparatory work by her online friends, *Grasshopper: The Poetry of M.A. Griffiths* was published by Arrowhead Press in 2011. It contains some remarkable poems, and is still in print.

This is a wonderful example of a poet who builds a readership without setting foot outside her house. It can be done. There are many ways. The key to them all is the connection with other human beings. During her lifetime, Grasshopper must have returned feedback on far more poems by other people than those she posted herself. She was a perceptive, critical and engaging reader. She was *interested* in what other people were doing. That interest was returned.

Write now: A word spell

CHOOSE THREE WORDS YOU particularly like the sound of. List them. Decide which one of the three you'd like to work with.

Write the word you've chosen large and clear on a big piece of paper in lower case. The piece of paper should be at least A4 in size, and the word should take up most of the space on the paper. You mustn't use any capital letters.

Trace round the letters of your word with the index finger of your writing hand, as though you're writing it again with your finger. Do this three times.

Look at the word so hard that when you close your eyes you can see it clearly.

Keep your eyes shut. Go inside the word. Walk up and down the letters one by one, as if you're a fly and the letters are as big as a bus. Fly through the loops as though they're windows. Think about the shapes and sounds as you go. Say the letters to yourself in your head.

Now you're a prisoner of this word. You're stuck inside it. You need a release spell to get you out.

Here's the spell that will release you. (You'll need another piece of paper.)

1. Write down three sentences with the word in it.
2. This will only take you a minute.
3. Read them aloud to underpin it.

Good. Now you're out.

Write about what it was like to be stuck inside that word. Where did that word take you?

Or any other idea that came out of this experience.

Chapter Seventeen: Performing your poems

LET'S SAY YOU DON'T *mind* reading in public. Perhaps you even like the idea. It is, after all, the best possible way to gauge how well the poems work out loud. Reading them to your dog is not the same.

But if you're going to do it, you need to do it well. This only comes with practice, which means on the first few occasions you may not be much good. But you will get better. Open mic events, or reading to fellow work-shoppers perhaps, will allow you to try things out, with the encouragement of an audience who won't mind if you're shy or fluff the last line.

I suggest that for *any* reading of your work you have your first and last poem by heart. I don't mean you should deliver them without the page (though performance poets often like to do this). I mean you should know them inside out, so if you lose your place you won't lose the next line because you'll *know* the last line. You'll also be able to look at the audience while you read the opening and closing phrases. If you look at the audience your voice will float up and out. If you look down at the paper, that's where your voice will go.

Reading poems aloud is a matter of giving the words, syllable by syllable, to the listeners. There they are, their little ears open and ready to receive. It's your job to make sure each part of each word gets there. Try thinking of them as people who can't quite hear properly. It's your bounden duty to help them.

You will need to read more slowly than you think.

You should *never* over-run your allotted time. Better to do the reverse and finish slightly early.

Poems start with silence and end with silence. It's the white space at the top and bottom of the page. Don't be afraid of that silence. Insist on it. It's part of the poem.

If your poem requires words of introduction, try writing those down too. You don't have to stick to what you've written precisely, but it means you'll say precisely what you need to say and no more, and you can measure in advance how long it takes.

Let's imagine you've just published a pamphlet of poems. Your local writers' group has invited you to come and read to them. What will make your reading a success?

Think about the way the brain processes aural information. People are going to hear each line only once. It's a million miles away from reading on the page, when the eye can jump back and forward at will.

Traditional aural forms (like songs and ballads) compensate for this by incorporating lots of repetition. If you hear the chorus or repeating phrase ten times, at least the key words connect.

Your poetry, however, may well be free verse, with no repetitive structures to help the ear. Your audience is going to have to concentrate hard to pick up every word and phrase. Introductions to poems and links between them are important. They allow the audience to get into correct listening mode, the equivalent of *Listen With Mother's* 'Are you sitting comfortably?' Listening well is hard. Listeners need all the help they can get.

Reading to an audience well isn't easy either, of course, but it's an art you can learn. Go and hear other poets or watch them on YouTube. Learn from what they do (or don't do), just as they have learned from others. But you might bear in mind the points on this list:

- Know your poems inside out and some of them off by heart.
- Practise at home. Time your reading.
- Prepare your links as well as your poems.
- Read more slowly than you think you need to.
- Don't forget to breathe.
- Make your mouth work: your lips and your tongue. Every single syllable needs to be heard.
- Look at the audience when you read your first and last lines.
- Before you start a poem, pause. When you end a poem, pause. Let the silence have its proper time.
- Look at your audience from time to time during the reading. If they can't hear you, or aren't following you, adjust speed or volume accordingly.
- Keep your sense of humour. If you totally duff up a poem, stop. Apologise. Start again. It will be fine.
- Not all poems work equally well out loud. Choose the ones that do.
- Stand proud. It's not about you, it's about the words. Trust them. If they're good ones, they will carry you.

MOST OF THE POEMS you read in magazines are non-fiction. By this I mean they're based on experience assumed to be true and often personal.

Most of the short stories and novels you read, however, are fiction – that is to say the characters and events are imaginary, though some of them may incorporate an element of truth.

For this writing slot, your poem should be based on an entirely invented person: pure fiction. If you have access to the internet, take yourself onto Google. Think of a person's name – not a person you know – make the name up. But it shouldn't be too extraordinary.

Put the name into Google search and then click 'images'. Various photos of people will come up, both genders. Pick just one. (If you can't manage Google + images, choose a photo from a magazine. Anyone will do, but give them a name.)

Here's your scenario. This person has lost something, and is keeping the loss secret. How do they feel about it? You need to spend some time with the photograph of your chosen person.

Right now, after googling 'Jonty Bloomsbury', I'm looking at a man in a tartan suit standing beside a bicycle, with one hand on the saddle. He has a beard and a tweed cap. The cap doesn't match the suit. The buttons on his jacket are on the tight side. He has an open-necked shirt and a cravat. He's standing squarely on two feet and his shoulders are back and his jaw is firm. I think I know what he's lost.

In your poem you could deal with the inner feelings of the person, or you could take them on a journey to find whatever it is. I don't think they will find it though. But they might find something else.

Play with this idea and see what happens. Poetry or prose – you decide.

Chapter Eighteen: How to get readings

'. . . a good friend of mine, who also happened to be the front-man in a band, asked me if I fancied doing a couple of poems before they went on. To this day I still don't why I agreed to it. When I got up, I performed the poems and shut my eyes and waited for the beer to start flying, but something totally unexpected happened. They applauded. They cheered.'

—Joe Hakim, from 'How I Accidentally Became a Spoken Word Poet',
sabotagetimes.com, 22 January 2013

A POET GETS A BOOK published and suddenly you see he or she is reading all over the place. How do such poets manage this?

It's all to do with relationships. They've been to other people's readings. They've supported events. They've made connections. They've done lots of open mic. They've made it clear they would like to read their work.

When they know they have a publication about to appear, they make contact with an event organiser and ask whether there might be a future slot for them. The organiser knows who they are because they've often been in the audience. So they're welcomed.

Or they're friendly with an established poet who does public events regularly. He or she has a reading coming up somewhere and suggests them as a second reader.

Or one of their Facebook friends is a poet who had a book published by the same publisher the previous year and then did a whole set of readings. They contact that person and ask them how they managed it. The poet offers to pass on their details to various event organisers.

Or the publisher recommends the poet to an event organiser. (If this happens, it will be because the publisher has heard that poet read and thought they were good. You only recommend someone for public performance if you know they perform well, and your favourite poet is not necessarily the best reader.)

Or the poet has been organising small readings in a local pub for years. He or she is an poetry event organiser. One event organiser respects another event organiser. Once a book comes out, such a poet is surprised by the invitations that pop up.

Or the poet contacts people via a social network like Facebook and asks friends for advice: have they any ideas about places to get readings? Brass neck sometimes goes a long way.

Or the poet (or their publisher) approaches a festival director, flagging up the fact that a new publication is imminent, from which the poet would be keen to read if a slot were available. But be careful. The world is full of poets who want to read at festivals, and it's no use just arriving out of the blue and expecting a red carpet. You have to do the preparation. You have to go to the festival yourself, as a punter. You have to check whether there are readings that feature 'new' poets, one of which might be suitable for you. You have to check the website for the right and wrong time of year to make contact. And for a festival, where normally you will be paid, the director will want to know you're a good reader because the whole festival stands or falls on selling tickets. How will you demonstrate this?

I talked about a magazine track record when approaching a publisher. There's a reading track record when approaching a festival director. You will have read at other, smaller events. If you're clear and memorable and arresting, the word will go round. You will harvest recommendations and sometimes someone in the audience will come up to you afterwards and invite you to read somewhere else. You may have the opportunity to make a recording. That, too, is helpful. Then, when you approach a festival director, you can offer a CD or DVD, or a YouTube link, or a SoundCloud link, or similar.

When you read, be remembered. I don't mean in a P.J. Proby trouser-splitting way, but there are small things you can do, none of which should be over-done. Obviously the best thing is to be remembered for performing good poems well. But sometimes you can plan something a little different. You might have a poem about a teddy that you had as a child, a very old teddy. You might produce the bear at the end of the poem. Or you might have a poem about the annoying ringtones of some smartphones, with a friend (or several) in the audience primed to make theirs sound during the opening line.

I will never forget hearing Russell Hoban read from his novel The Mouse and His Child. He brought with him the clockwork toy at the heart of the book. He wound it up, placed it on a table, and the father mouse went round and round and round holding the child mouse up high. The applause was deafening.

Why would you do all this? It's all part of getting the work out there, finding the readers, building a readership. You've published one book, do you think you might ever hope to do it again? If so, the first book is going to have to sell.

But you may also have fun. Poets are allowed this too.

Case Study

A poet sends not just a few poems with a proposal but a whole pamphlet carefully presented on A5 pages (printed at home and folded so the poems fall as they would in published format) with a title page, acknowledgements page, contents, page numbers on all 32 pages, bio for jacket, quotations from notable poets for back cover, and a full colour photograph for a painting to go on the front. The title for the collection (it is not a *proposed* title, it is *the* title) is *Morning Mourning*.

What a horrible title! But that's beside the point. This is just not how I do things. Being presented with a whole publication before we've even agreed I like his poems well enough to publish – this is not my idea of an editor's role.

I look inside. Yes, I like the work. Good writing. And grief is a central theme but it doesn't smack you in the eye or anything: much more subtle than the title suggests. That title would *have* to go! But I have the feeling this poet has decided what he wants. This is his pamphlet and he thinks my job is to reject or accept, then print it. But I'm not a printer. I'm a publisher.

I could explain this to him, as well as the fact that I don't do colour covers or blurby quotations on the back, but it will get complicated and sound like a half-offer of publication. What I'd really like to do is wind him back in time to before he sent the stuff at all, and say 'just send me twelve poems' and we'll see.

But I have too many publications on my plate anyway, so I return the work with a note: 'It was a pleasure to read your poems and thank you for sending them. I liked a number of them, especially 'Fig Pudding' and 'Tender is the Day', but I didn't fall in love with the set as a whole so regret I can't offer to work with you on this occasion.'

I don't mention submission guidelines. I am feeling so repetitive these days . . .

Write now: Poems with props

Have you ever heard someone using that phrase 'putting on one of my other hats'? A person says it when they're just about to change role. They might, for example, be a teacher by profession but also the chair of the local gardening association. So they might precede a comment about the state of your roses, with 'putting on my gardening hat'.

I'm suggesting you might write a poem in which you put on a number of hats. The poem might be about your various roles in life, referred to as hats. When you've written it, you might think about *actual* hats. Could you perform this poem and put on a new hat with each stanza? It's a nice idea. Think about it.

Knitting as a metaphor for life. Can you knit? My mother could knit, talk and watch television all at the same time. Could you write a poem that draws on knitting language (back to the talk of your trade)? In fact, you might write a poem in which knitting forms a kind of refrain:

> I saw him last night. He looked in here
> on his way back from the King's Arms
> *knit one purl one*
>
> I said to him, 'One too many, is it?'
> but he was already too far gone
> *knit one purl one*

The speaker at the heart of this would, of course, be a knitter. When you came to perform the poem, you would take your knitting with you. You would be a sensation.

There are so many possibilities for a poem with props. A poem about disguise. A poem about wigs. A poem about a particular childhood toy. A poem about a balloon as a symbol for vain hope. (You have a pin secreted in one hand. After the last line you pop the balloon.)

Give the matter some thought. It could be fun.

Chapter Nineteen: Workshopping – yes or no?

'Making mistakes in their choice of what to take on is one of the things that publishers do, and always have done. Despite all the research data now available, no one really knows which books will find many thousands of readers and which only a handful. I'd argue that the freedom to make mistakes constitutes the chief glory of the profession.'

—Charles Boyle in 'The Freedom to Fail', *The Literary Review*, September 2015

ONCE A POET SENT me a submission of poems and in her covering letter she said they were unlikely to need editing because they had all been 'thoroughly workshopped'. This somehow reminded me of processed cheese or spam. I felt quite sorry for the poems.

On another occasion, my feedback to a poet differed from the guidance he had followed from a workshop leader, and he pointed this out in no uncertain terms. This is delicate. Different people think different things, and it's good to know how each of them responds to your work and mainly useful. But *you* are the one who has to decide what's right for your poems. No-one else will do.

Of course it's not essential to join a workshop and expose your poems to practical criticism (or praise). However, if you find the right group (and this isn't always easy), it may help a lot. The whole process of group membership is about more than just your poems: it's about you having the confidence to comment on other people's work and bounce ideas around. It's about learning.

There are also poetry *reading* groups, where members bring in and discuss other people's poems. Some groups discuss all the books on the T. S. Eliot Prize shortlist! If you're reluctant to expose your own poems to a workshop session, a reading group might be something you'd prefer and enjoy. It's also the kind of group you could start yourself if there isn't one near you.

For me, workshopping played a crucial role. But there were no such things as poetry workshops in my local area when I was first looking for one. So I joined one online. The one I used nearly twenty years ago still exists. It's called the Internet Writing Workshop and it has 'critiquing lists' for all genres. Membership is free and the poetry list has up to 60 active members at any one time (you have to be active to stay in the group). I still think the way it works is excellent, though like any other group, you will feel a connection with some members and not others. The workshop isn't just about sharing poems. You can start poetry discussion topics there, or contribute to them.

But it is a serious matter to join. You do it if you're working hard at your writing and want feedback. I think the IWW principles are as sound as they come:

> 'While poetry submitted for critique is often free verse, we adventure to embrace new and traditional genres of poetry. Members challenge and encourage one another to explore the unfamiliar, yet aim to support and respect the individual's voice.'

The IWW poetry list participants do this while striving not to fall 'into the dreaded trap that some editors call 'workshop' or 'cookie-cutter' poetry.' You have to agree to critique and/or submit poems a minimum of eight times per month (roughly twice a week). If you don't do that, you lose your place in the group. This doesn't mean you're posting eight poems a month. Far from it. Although you contribute at least eight times per month, most of your contributions will be in the form of feedback on other people's poems. You can critique as many poems as you like. But when it comes to your own writing, you're only allowed to submit one poem at a time, and you have to wait at least a week before sending another.

The emphasis is less on the critiques you *get* than on those you *give*. Properly considered critiques are essential. Just saying 'I like it' is no use. You have to point out which lines appealed and say why, or vice versa. There's a whole etiquette involved in this, and it takes a little while to get your head around it. The IWW has voluntary administrators who intercede tactfully if there seems to be a problem or someone gets it wrong.

During my time in that workshop, I learned more from critiquing other people's poems than anything else. It was immeasurably educative. When critiques came back on my own work, I quickly learned which 'critters' made useful points and which could be safely ignored. New people regularly joined the list, posted a couple of poems and then never re-appeared. They wanted to get (positive) feedback but not give it. But in other cases, I began to feel critiques and poems were by people I knew personally, and their feedback was invaluable.

To return the favour, I took more and more pride in giving thoughtful critiques. Some of the poems were absolutely fascinating. The fact that we were based in many different parts of the English-speaking world was a wonderful added extra – so many influences and ways of approaching poetry!

This kind of group doesn't create cookie-cutter poems. Such things are more likely to be produced as a result of a set exercise, perhaps with a whole set of friends attempting it together. I confess I do sometimes read poems where I think I can guess the workshop idea that gave rise to the text. But a good poem will always travel far from its original stimulus, because a good poem isn't like any other poem, unless it deliberately tries to be (parody is a case in point). It's possible sometimes that poet friends may start to use similar forms, but it's only one of many risks attendant on any writer, and a new participant in the group can soon upset that particular apple-cart.

I spent a couple of years working in IWW (at the same time as sending poems off to magazines). During that time some of the participants became friends, and personal correspondences developed off-list. My poet friends were now all over the world: one in Australia, one in New Zealand, one in California, a couple in London, one in India. Eventually, I left the Internet Writing Workshop and joined a splinter group of former members. We called ourselves 'Corners' because we were in all corners of the globe and because of John Donne's holy sonnet 'At the round earth's imagin'd corners, blow / Your trumpets, angels'.

Eventually, Corners dissolved. A poetry group, like any other group, has its day. People need to move on. There's a natural tendency in any group towards conformity, and poetry is not a natural conformer, nor should it ever be.

I remain in touch with five former IWW members and number two of them among my closest friends.

Write now: The earworm

—Mark Twain

SOMETIMES SOMEONE SAYS SOMETHING to you that sticks in your head and goes round and round and round. Sometimes you hear that particular phrase, whatever it is, for the rest of your life. It pops up at odd times.

It might be a time when someone put you in your place, or gave you advice, or lied to you. The time a loved one broke up with you. Phrases that really hurt us tend to stay with us.

So do words said in poignant situations: the last thing your dad said before he died.

Or perhaps it's a cliché? When my sister and I fought as children my grandmother used to say, 'Don't let the sun go down on your wrath.' That's how I learned what 'wrath' meant. Some things stick.

Allow this idea to work away in your mind. Note down any phrases you remember. I know you have some! The more you think about it the more will pop up, so give yourself time.

Many of mine are things my mother said, and I did put one into a poem. Here it is. The earworm is line three. But your task is to use one, or more than one, of such phrases from your own life in a completely different poem.

Preferences

'Well, one thing is perfectly certain,'
my mother said, putting down her iron,
'men prefer to marry a virgin.'

It was something I'd already heard.
She'd taught me, though, how silly my father was.
Who cared what he preferred?

Helena Nelson, from *Unsuitable Poems*, HappenStance 2005

Chapter Twenty: Putting a collection together

'But I do think that a lot of books are published not because they're wonderful, but because they're fairly safe bets. They're books that are similar to what sold well the year before, or they are like so-and-so crossed with so-and-so.'

—CB Editions editor Charles Boyle interviewed by James Tookey
for 3:am Magazine, 14 October 2015

SO YOU'VE ACQUIRED A body of work. A good number of your poems, perhaps all of them, have been published in reputable magazines. You move the furniture in your study to make as much space as you can on the floor. You lay all the poems out. What have you got? How on earth are you going to make them look like a book?

I think of a book as having three possible aspects. There's the idea of the book – the key concept the reader might get hold of before even reading it. Then there's the book itself with all its component pages and whatever happens inside them. Finally there's the story of the book: how it gradually came together, how it found a publisher, what happened after it was printed and fell into the hands of readers.

The key concept, which might – in some circumstances – be described as a USP (unique selling point or proposition) – may be important in catching the attention of readers to whom the author's name means little or nothing. In 2013, HappenStance Press published a pamphlet by Diana Gittins titled *Bork!* The poems inside all featured hens, in one context or another, most of them the birds loved and reared by the author. At the start of the pamphlet a page announced 'The pop hole is open', and at the end 'The pop hole is closed'. Above each poem, where a title might have been, there was a chicken's footprint.

Diana had participated in more than one poetry group and had loyal poetry friends. So she was able to organise a publication launch, at which sales were brisk. Many people who knew her name and work also ordered a copy. But most interestingly there were numerous sales to people who weren't familiar with her work but simply kept chickens. Somehow the word had reached them. A good number of orders for were for two copies at once, because people who keep chickens frequently know other people who do the same. Until this point, I had no idea that so many many poets kept hens!

So this pamphlet achieved its USP effortlessly. I'm not suggesting you should write a set of poems about chickens. Or goldfish. Or knitting. It's just that sometimes there is a unifying concept right under your nose. When you read Diana's poems – like all other poems – they're about far more than they're about. Chickens are the least of it.

Back to your poems on the floor looking up at you reproachfully. Get a piece of paper. Make a list of recurring themes. There might be five that touch on your father's death for example, and six gardening poems; four about your grandchildren, two about toothache. What is the balance like? Are there poems that naturally group together? Or do they need splitting up?

Readers tend to make their own narratives out of books. They tend to start at the beginning and put together a version of events as they go through. We like stories. You can play to this by starting with poems about your early life and then following through in a sort of chronological arc. Many debut collections do this.

Or you might feel there were four or five life 'stories' in the book, and you could group them, or interweave them.

Or you could decide the idea of journeys was central to your book and you could group the poems according to journey, or continent, or method of travel.

Or the poems might seem to fit naturally into four seasons: Spring, Summer, Autumn, Winter.

Or the poems might be mainly love stories: love for people, pets, cars, mountains.

Or you might find the idea of good luck and bad luck runs right through like the writing in a stick of rock. (You might tweak a couple of poem titles to sharpen this idea.)

You may want to call in a friend to help with organising the poems, because other people see things you don't. Once you start to spot a thread emerging, you may find two 'must-have-in-my-book' poems don't seem to belong. They may not fit. You may need to hold them back for your second book. When you have a publisher, ask her or his opinion. You would really like to have fitted this poem in, but you couldn't find a place for it. What does she or he think?

There's a huge difference between a set of poems and a collection. I believe a collection does ideally need a characterising factor, and the title will bind to it. So one of the things you be doing now is noticing book titles. Which ones are memorable? Which are instantly forgettable?

When you approach your publisher, it's no bad thing if you already have a concept idea for your book. If you haven't, the publisher may try to come up with one and you may not like it much. A working idea of concept may also strengthen what you write and how you write it during your months (or years) of preparation. The concept sits at the heart of the book blurb. It goes in the advance information sheet sent out to reps and competitions and events. It's part of the press release, the email newsletter, the Facebook announcement. It may even be what Chris Hamilton-Emery calls 'Your Thirty-Second Sell', of which one superb sentence will be 'The One Sentence Hard Sell'.

(I sense your teeth clenching and your heart sinking. Try to enjoy this. You are a poet. You don't have to take marketing language seriously but you *do* have to take the language in which your book is described very seriously indeed.)

So start collecting book blurbs that work. Set up a Google alert for 'poetry debut' and the notifications will drop into your email box. Here's one that popped into mine only this week (February 2016) about Miriam Bird Greenberg, a US poet who won the 2015 Agnes Lynch Starrett Poetry Prize with *In the Volcano's Mouth*. Here's the description of her forthcoming book from the website of the *Houston Chronicle*:

'The collection draws from Greenberg's adventures hitchhiking, bicycling and crossing the continent on freight trains. Along the way, she encountered modern nomads, hobos and other individuals living on the socioeconomic edge.'

Does this sound different? Does it sound like the poems add up? I think so. What about *The Old Weird Albion*, a debut collection from American writer and artist Justin Hopper, due out from Penned in the Margins, 2016? The title is intriguing, and here's the brief description on the publisher's blog:

'In *The Old Weird Albion*, American writer and artist Justin Hopper will set forth into the foggy underculture of the South Downs Way in search of an alternate version of English identity. Taking in urban spaces, suburbs and sweeping landscapes in the

Sussex homeland of Hopper's ancestors, this debut will attempt to reconnect with the land and the self.'

Does it sound different? Does it sound like the poems add up? I believe it does. I suggest you take a look at some other poetry debuts for yourself. You might, for example, check out Annie Freud's 2007 debut from Picador, *The Best Man That Ever Was*, or Shazea Quraishi, *The Art of Scratching* (Bloodaxe, 2015) and Hannah Lowe's *Chick* (Bloodaxe, 2013). Read the book descriptions on jackets and websites. Reflect.

How does all this help you with those poems spread out across the floor? If we were to throw your book into the set we considered so far, how could we describe it? What's going on in your poems? What's the driving force?

I have no recipe for what your poems should be doing. There *is* no 'should'. But I suspect various aspects of style, form and content give your work individuality. It's for you to work out how this might attract readers (and in the first instance, a publisher). If you told me your poems drew on memories of your mother during her illness and eventual death, I might feel this was all too familiar territory. But if you said your mother was married to a spy during the Second World War, and your book drew on the way she came to terms with this during her illness, now *that* would be quite something. If you told me your poems reflected the natural world in all its moods, I would probably think 'Oh dear' (sorry). But if you told me your poems dealt with the polarities of the natural world – brutal violence and devastating beauty – I would give you my full attention.

Suppose you're entering a pamphlet competition – does the set of poems require a central theme or binding concept? In an interview in 2011, I asked Peter Sansom of The Poetry Business what the likely ingredients for a winning pamphlet might be, and this is what he said:

'Good poems are always the key. Don't worry about sequencing or subject matter. Just write good poems.'

Of course if you were to win that competition, the editors would help you present the resulting publication in the best possible way.

I don't begin to suggest this is easy.

Convalescence

And so I took a stone to weigh it in my hands
and then another, lighter or heavier, to weigh also,
and in this balancing of stone against stone
moved through the morning easily, approaching noon
with the light sweat of simple achievement. And soon,
uncertainly, began to place the stones, began
a circle wider than I had intended, into which
nevertheless I stepped at last
to take account of myself, to stand and wonder.

Peter Gilmour, from *Taking Account*, HappenStance 2011

THE TITLE AND THE last line of Peter Gilmour's poem make you wonder whether the circle of stones is real or metaphorical. I think it might be both, but of course I don't know.

Certainly, this is a good example of a poem in which the title makes an enormous difference. Suppose the poem was called 'Stone Circle'? I think it would read very differently. Suppose it was called 'Citadel', or 'Beach Holiday' – again, what a difference! But no. It's 'Convalescence', from which we infer the speaker has been ill, either physically or mentally or both. The phrase 'take account of myself' at the end seems pregnant with meaning. One can't be sure what is going on, although in another sense it is perfectly clear. The narrator is building a ring of stones, perhaps a circular wall. If it is a wall, it's not very high, because he steps inside at the end.

I think it's a compelling poem, perhaps because of the way all physical action has a mental correlation. When I tidy my desk and clear all the papers into tidy piles, I am also doing something in my head. When I describe my actions precisely, I begin to feel I understand something I didn't know before.

So here's your poem task. Simply describe a set of actions you might undertake. You might be stacking logs, or planting out daffodil bulbs, or stapling paper. It must be something you do often, so you

105

can describe it literally and clearly. This is your poem. The first line should begin 'Afterwards'. The poem should be nine lines long and the penultimate line should be shorter than all the rest.

When you're done, think about titles carefully. You'll find a list of abstract nouns in brackets below. Choose one of them for your title (but not until after you've written the poem) or a different one that you like better.

(Preparation, Attempt, Undoing, Calculation, Love, Heroism, Faith, Care, Neglect, Ambition, Allocation, Indolence, Hedonism, Altruism, Barbarity, Age.)

Chapter Twenty-One: Self-publishing

'Reading back, I wonder if I have given a false impression of all work and no play. Though the one-man publisher may work harder and for more hours in the year than Incorporated Man, he can at least allot them according to whim, weather and opportunity.'

—Jon Wynne-Tyson from *Finding the Words, A Publishing Life*,
Michael Russell Publishing Ltd, 2004

SELF-PUBLISHING IS NOT THE same thing as vanity publishing. Vanity publishing is a way of making money out of authors. If you find this confusing, which it frequently is, consult Johnathon Clifford's website (www.vanitypublishing.info). He points out, among other things, that 'mainstream publishers do not advertise for authors'. He also offers a free and extremely helpful advice pack.

Poets get fed up with the whole poetry publishing malarkey. Of course they do. Many decide to take the matter into their own hands. Self-publishing is a perfectly honourable option, especially for work that wouldn't easily find a publisher.

My first HappenStance pamphlet was a self-publication, mainly of humorous poems. I already had a first full collection in print, and I was doing a fair number of readings. I thought I could probably flog enough copies of *Unsuitable Poems* to cover my costs.

More importantly, I thought if I made a mess of my first attempt at publishing, it would be better to do that with my own work than someone else's. It was a learning experience. (You might note that the book you are reading at this very minute is also self-published, just as Chris Hamilton-Emery's *101 Ways to Make Poems Sell* was brought out through Salt Publishing, his own imprint.)

Self-publishing can be done well. All you have to do is possess, beg or borrow the necessary skills and pay for the printing (and possibly type-setting). You will also need to find out the legal deposit requirements but this is not complicated. If you buy an ISB number all the instructions come with it, and if you don't, there are no rules: you can do what you like with the copies. All of them.

At the time of writing, self-published poetry pamphlets are eligible for The Michael Marks Award for Poetry Pamphlets, and in Scotland for the Callum MacDonald Memorial Award. They are also eligible for the Poetry Book Society quarterly pamphlet choice.

Suppose you were a performance poet, doing regular gigs and in a position to sell dozens of sets of publications at each event. Why ask someone else to publish them? If you do it yourself, you foot the bill but you also pocket every penny of the returns from sales.

You might feel self-publication confers less kudos. There's some truth in this, though things have changed in the last decade, and eligibility of self-published pamphlets for some awards reflects this. The big challenge for the self-publisher, as for the professional publisher, is to find a readership for the book. But a self-publisher who typesets her- or himself and prints cheaply could afford to give the first 100 copies away (as is sometimes done for ebooks) and could then send out review copies to appropriate magazines. Thereafter, would readers enjoy and ask for more? Whether you sell your book or give it away, that's the question you need to ask yourself.

What if you approach a book publisher with a full collection and you already have a self-published pamphlet in print? Will it put them off? Why should it? If the self-publication has already attracted appreciative readers and been part of creating a demand for more, it can only be to the good.

Case Study

A packet of 45 poems arrives with a charming letter (outside my reading window). A fellow publisher has just turned them down for a book but has said a smaller set would make an excellent pamphlet, and has recommended Happen*Stance*. He has assured her I am 'good at working with poets to develop a fine publication'. Ha! The fellow publisher has not offered to publish the fine publication, I note. I can't read these poems now. I haven't time to eat breakfast, let alone read 45 poems.

The author hasn't checked out the reading windows on my website. Nor has she, so far as I know, read any Happen*Stance* publications, let alone bought one. She is thinking like a poet, not like a publisher.

Not surprising, really. She hasn't read *How (not) to Get Your Poetry Published*, so I had better finish writing it.

This Living Hand

This living hand, now warm and capable
Of earnest grasping, would, if it were cold
And in the icy silence of the tomb,
So haunt thy days and chill thy dreaming nights
That thou wouldst wish thine own heart dry of blood
So in my veins red life might stream again,
And thou be conscience-calmed – see here it is –
I hold it towards you.

John Keats, written in the margin of another, longer poem, probably
near the end of 1819. He died in February 1821.

CAN YOU READ THIS Keats poem without first a little shudder and second, a glance at your own hands?

How often do you look at your own hands carefully? When I look at mine. I'm shocked by how old they are, how translucent the skin, how veiny. Not what I expect to see at all. But John Keats's hand was that of a young man in his twenties.

Visual artists make studies of hands. And Michelangelo's image of God's hand reaching out to Adam's at the moment of creation on the ceiling of the Sistine Chapel is, of course, iconic.

Poets write with hands, but they don't often write about them.

But this is your task now. Just take one hand, the hand you write with. Look at it carefully. Describe.

Then do something in the poem that reaches out to the reader. I don't know what. You decide.

Chapter Twenty-two: Some 'what ifs'

'There is also no one-size-fits-all way to be a writer. There never has been.'

—Charles Boyle, SonofaBook blog, August 2015

W HAT IF YOUR POEM isn't like anything on *any* publisher's list? What if your poem is three hundred feet long and consists of one word per line? What if your poem has to be sung? What if your poem is entirely derived from sources also used by T. S. Eliot in 'The Waste Land' and makes no sense unless you also read 'The Waste Land'? What if none of your work has ever been printed in any magazine ever because it simply doesn't fit?

You don't have to be like the rest. Sometimes the exception is more interesting by virtue of being different. But if you want the work published, start looking for a publisher who is as original as you. It is not likely to be one of the big ones.

W HAT IF YOUR BOOK has been accepted by the publisher, the contract is signed, you've told all your friends and . . . the publisher goes bust?

You will be upset. Of course, you will. A box of hankies or a bottle of decent wine, depending on preference, may be required. However, you are not back to square one. One publisher was sufficiently interested to commit. Now you have to decide who else to try, with this as a useful addition to your selling points and a necessary detail in your approach letter. If you had a plan to start with, you can go back to it and see who was next on your list. Unless the publisher has asked you to, you don't need to keep this blow secret. Telling people could be useful, because it's always possible another interested publisher might get in touch. (In the last resort, if you go for self-publishing, at least you will always be able to say the book was to have been published by X and you yourself stepped into the fray.)

W HAT IF YOUR BOOK finally appears in print and the publisher has made a pig's breakfast of it? The background colour on the jacket is yellow, not dark green as originally agreed. You notice (too late) that the Contents page is all wrong: it lists three poems that were dropped and the page numbers have been missed out. And one of the poems inside has been printed so that the first word of each line disappears into the inside margin.

This is not good, I agree. But you have some responsibility here. At the proofing stage, you should have had an opportunity to notice these things. Did you? If you weren't supplied with a proof you have good cause to grumble, but if you were, and you didn't say? It's important to remember that people are dying and suffering all over the world at this very minute, in circumstances worse than yours. This is not the end of the world. It is the beginning of a learning experience for you. You can approach the publisher and politely point out the errors, and she or he may agree to reprint the volume. If this happens, all is well. If it doesn't, you will make the best of it, while quietly sharing the facts with other poets you trust. Reputation is important for publishers: this one has just gone down a peg or two with you and your friends.

When you do readings, you can make the errors into a joke for sharing with the audience. If there is a reprint, in which these errors are corrected, you can declare that the erroneous version will be worth money for its interest and rarity in decades to come. When you read aloud the poem that disappears into the margin, you could do it twice: once as a challenge with the first word of each line missing. Then again in the way it *should* sound. Ask the audience which version they prefer? If it's a friendly setting, you may get an additional round of applause.

But of course, you may not want to go back to that publisher with your second collection.

WHAT IF YOU HAVE a second collection ready and, for one reason or another, you can't get it published by the imprint that did it the first time?

You're going to have to approach another publisher. However, a key factor this time is how well your first book did. You need to be able to suggest that sales have been healthy, and that you've been out and about making connections, doing readings, building your readership. If the whole experience was a disaster, and you only sold 50 copies, you can't approach another publisher blaming the last one for lost sales. It will make them very nervous. But perhaps the first collection, now you look back on it, was a mistake. You did it too soon and the contents were not that great. You regret it, in fact. You might consider working towards a strong pamphlet, rather than a second book at this stage.

WHAT IF YOU HAVE no USP? What if nothing characterises your set of poems other than the fact that you wrote them?

If they are good enough, this won't matter. Also an editor may see a USP that's too obvious for you to notice it.

WHAT IF YOU HAVE enraged your publisher by trying to change aspects of the collection, including rewriting some of the poems, sixteen times between first offer and printing?

Try not to do this. Relationships are important, and there is a time to let go. If you want to rewrite poems at the last minute, do it later and make a feature of it. Publish a volume titled *The B side: rewrites of A.* Better still, write some new ones.

WHAT IF YOU AND your publisher can't agree about the contents of your first collection? You have a set of villanelles you think must go in. The publisher thinks the villanelles weaken all the other poems and wants you to leave them out. The publisher wants 64 pages. You want 80.

Ultimately the publisher has last call on this. She or he makes an offer on a set of poems they like. They are paying for the resulting book and they will be trying to sell it. They will try to work *with* you, not against you, but if you insert poems in which they have no confidence, they don't have to go ahead. If you're determined to have these villanelles in, come what may, you'll need to find another publisher, or publish the book yourself.

WHAT IF YOU WRITE light verse? What if you like to be funny?

I love good light verse and so do hundreds of people. There are regular competitions for it in *The Spectator, The Oldie* and *The New Statesman,* and a whole coterie of poets contribute regularly. They set a high standard and if you want to compete, you'd better take it seriously. You'll also find some of their work in the ezine *Lighten-Up Online*. What you *won't* often find is debut collections of light verse. I don't remember the last one I saw.

Why should this be? At readings, the funny poems often go down best. When it comes to sales, the witty collections – unless they're by tried and tested old favourites like Roger McGough and Pam Ayres, Wendy Cope and Spike Milligan – are not impressive. As Happen*Stance* editor, I have published two pamphlets of light verse, one by Martin Parker, the other by Graham Austin. I loved them both. Both authors were actively involved in public readings in their local areas, and Martin was founder editor of *Lighten-Up Online*. Don't get me wrong: these publications found a warm and welcoming readership. But overall, the pamphlets sold more slowly than others with sober styles.

I don't recall a funny or even mildly witty poem ever winning the National Poetry Competition. I don't believe a pamphlet of light verse has ever been a Poetry Book Society quarterly recommendation. So far as I know, no witty set of pamphlet poems has ever been shortlisted for the Michael Marks Award for pamphlet poetry, or if it was, I missed it. What does this say about us? I'm not sure. But many poets are wary of writing humorously in case it should mean they're not taken seriously. And they may be right. Humour is an odd phenomenon: what one person thinks hilarious, another thinks bad taste.

There are poets such as John Whitworth and Ann Drysdale, and sometimes even myself, who publish witty verse mingled with more serious poems. This is a hard balance to get right and new young poets tend not even to try to be funny. I don't know why. Poetry World can, I sometimes think, destroy a perfectly good sense of humour if you let it. But it may also be that being funny without being reductive is the hardest thing of all. Irony is quite another matter.

If you can become famous *enough*, of course, you can do what you like. You can, like T. S. Eliot, do both 'The Four Quartets' and *Old Possum's Book of Practical Cats*.

But poets lower down the slopes of Parnassus will find it harder to place a collection of light verse than almost any other kind.

Write now: An offer you can't refuse

'Ready-made ideas of how things should be done are useful, for creative thinking is very tiring and it is sometimes a relief to be given a rest from it, but ultimately, every person must devise his or her own way of making sense out of the confusing business of being alive."

—Alison Prince, from *The Necessary Goat & Other Essays on Formative Thinking*, Taranis Books, 1992

YOU GET AN EMAIL making you a wonderfully attractive offer. But you're going to refuse, though the person who has made you the offer will find this impossible to believe.

I don't know what the offer is or why you *have* to refuse, but it's absolutely essential that you do. This will cause you pain.

Write a poem of refusal.

Use your own scenario.

Accommodation

Yes, that part of me is reserved.
It is a sleeping chrysalis
between the neatly folded towels
in the airing cupboard, alone
in the warm dark. It has gone
to where a woman keeps her work.

No. Neither for your open vowels
nor brown eyes that have observed
much, will I tender this.

Helena Nelson, from *Plot and Counter-plot*, Shoestring Press 2010

Chapter Twenty-three: Spoken word

'... I try to work with poets who gig gig gig gig gig. Poets who work and work and see the book as something incremental to their offer are walking, talking one person marketing campaigns. People like to buy a book direct from the writer. I aim to navigate a path that adds value to the poet. Poets tell me that having a book published by Burning Eye helps them get booked for more of the bigger performance venues and festivals. Poets who get booked by the bigger performance venues and festivals sell more books.'

—Clive Birnie of Burning Eye Books talking to Will Barrett,
PubChat interviews, campus.poetryschool.com

WHEN YOU READ (OR PERFORM) your poems to an audience, it's a kind of publication in itself. You're sharing your words, broadcasting them for people to make of them what they will. There's often an assumed distinction between 'performance poets' and the rest, but all poets can aspire to performance, just as all performance poets can want their work on the printed page. It is not a question of either/or. You can have both.

There are, nevertheless, vastly different styles of performance. Some performers read from books or paper. Most perform from memory. It's not just about the words. Elements of theatre, dance, mime and poetry may be drawn in.

Then of course, there's competitive slam. If you think you might be interested, there's a huge amount of recorded material on the web: the full range can be sampled at will. Here, half the fun is in working an audience – in itself a skill, and one that can be learned if you have the verve and the aptitude. It tends to be associated with the young but that's just a stereotype: some older poets are first-rate slammers.

But what about the approach to publishing for 'spoken word' poets? I mentioned earlier that a popular performer may want to self-publish, and there's a good case for this, because it maximises profit from sales. But the poet may want an editor, someone who can tidy up text and help it to work on the page as well as possible. Not all poets are great at punctuation, grammar or spelling. If this applies to you, you need a good and literate editor. A reputable imprint can also bring you kudos and help you get better gigs. In the end, you may be in this business to make a living, something that page poets can't pretend to, although the attendant activities they sometimes engage in, such as teaching and residencies, may generate income.

There are imprints that specialise in spoken word publication. Nasty Little Press did this for several years but has bowed out now. Burning Eye books moved into the market in 2012. There are others who willingly support and publish writers who primarily see themselves as spoken word artists. If you want to see what the options are, it's simple. Go and hear some of the most successful performers, preferably live but if you can't manage that, online. Get hold of their published work. Who did the job? How well have they done it? Is there an opening here for you? Remember there are many ways of publishing, and not all of them involve paper: there's film, there's sound file, there's song lyric, there's 'Chinese Whispers'.

And meanwhile, just like the printed word poets, the job is simple. Whether it's a readership or an audience that you're creating, the steps are the same. Study your art. Study the artists you admire. Work out how they got published: there will be many models. Choose the one most likely to work for you and then analyse the necessary next steps.

Case Study

A nice email asking for advice from an aspiring poet. She's doing lots of performance work herself (no publication to her name but it sounds like she's enjoying herself) and she also runs a youth group developing performance skills in young people. She would like to get a pamphlet of their work into print, can I help.

The trouble is – answering takes time. There are all sorts of things she can do, and of course she can make this publication happen. But it depends what skills she can muster, who she knows and what kind of budget she has. I can't offer to do it myself: I don't take on this kind of publication.

There are other people she might have approached more usefully than me. Perhaps someone has told her I'm nice. I *am* nice, or at least I used to be, but I'm incredibly pressed for time and there are an awful lot of emails. I send her a brief reply with some names, some links and a good luck message.

Write now: Banishing writer's block

'We have Creativity on Friday afternoons,' a Headmistress told me once. 'The children are too tired by then to do any proper work.'

—Alison Prince, from *The Necessary Goat & Other Essays on Formative Thinking*, Taranis Books, 1992

I DON'T BELIEVE IN WRITER'S block. I think it's an invention. There are reasons why people sometimes find it difficult to write – if they feel very sad, for example. Or if they simply don't have the right kind of time.

But your challenge now is to make time for creating poems. You don't need to apply for a month on some writers' retreat. All you need is determination. Try this for one week.

Set aside two hours per day. If possible these two hours should be the same two hours. If you can't manage two, make it one. If you have to get up one hour earlier each day to make this happen, so be it.

Make sure you have all you need to write comfortably: the sort of pen or laptop you like, the sort of paper, a comfortable chair, good light, and no interruptions. This is *your* time. No-one else is allowed to interrupt.

Before the week begins, select your starting line, which should be any line from a contemporary poem. If you don't have time to look for one, take this one from Tom Duddy's 'Night Rain' in *The Years*: 'I turn to look one more time . . .'.

On day one, start writing, continuing from your given line. Keep writing without stopping for at least ten minutes, no matter what rubbish comes out. Then slow down, and write in whatever way you like, whatever you want. When you come to the end of your time, make sure you're in the middle of something. On day two, pick up where you left off. Each day, stop before something is properly finished.

Every day for seven days you're going to write. Try not to revise so much as write new things and more of them. You could tackle some of the writing ideas from this book. Or you could pick up an idea from your notebook and run with it. If you get stuck, choose another line from another poem, write it down and then keep going.

On the last day of the week, bring to your table one beautiful thing and one ugly thing. Set them in front of you. Why is one beautiful? What makes the other ugly? Write about the ugly thing as though it is beautiful and the beautiful thing as though it is ugly.

The week is over. Time to go back to the things you wrote. Revise them, stretch them, hone them, prune them, extend them, burn them. Do whatever needs to be done.

No such thing as writer's block.

Chapter Twenty-four: Afterword

'And so, if our life as a publisher fails to offer sufficient opportunities for laughter, this means it's just not serious enough.'

—Roberto Calasso, *The Art of the Publisher*, Penguin Books 2015, tr. Richard Dixon

THIS BOOK MAY HAVE put you off the whole idea of getting your poetry published. At times, I agree the whole business seems antithetical to the idea of writing. But it's not my intention to put you off. Not in the least.

Working on an actual poem when the idea comes to you and you're excited by the act of making – this is *so* much more enjoyable than putting a whole collection together! I know it all too well. But encouraging a set of poems to 'talk to each other' is creative too. In some ways, everything you write is part of the same thing. It did, after all, come out of the same brain. But the order in which you assemble it, the choices about what to highlight and lowlight, what to include and what to leave out – these are artistic decisions. It's perhaps not a million miles from working on a poem. If stanzas are the subsections of poems, poems are the subsections of the bigger poem which is the book. A book has only one title: the eye-catching umbrella under which everything happily shelters.

If you arrive at a collection you like – if you arrive at a collection you're proud of – there will be a way of getting it published and sharing it with a wider readership. There is always a way, though you may have to be open-minded about which one and consider options you hadn't originally thought of.

My first self-published pamphlet was done at home. (I didn't think of it as 'publishing'.) I word processed it and printed it at work (after hours) on A4 paper which I could fold in half to make A5 pages. I sewed the booklet in the middle with green embroidery thread, until I got bored with that and borrowed a long stapler from Reprographics. The covers were dark green paper, also stolen. I made twenty copies to give away to friends and family, especially my mother – the one who thought I 'ought' to have some poetry published. This was before I was involved in the public side of poetry, and before I had got far with sending poems to magazines. This little publication was called *With My Mother Missing The Train & Other Poems*. I still have a couple of copies of *Missing the Train* (which will never appear in a bibliographical record). Later some of the poems inside it, or versions of them, were included in my first book.

Not all writing has any connection with publishing. Other *Missing the Train* poems never went anywhere, for the best of reasons, though I know where they are and where they took me, and that's fine too.

But now – if getting a collection published is dear to your heart – it's time for you to start (or finish) your action plan. There are workbook pages for doing precisely that.

Equally, you could use them to write new poems.

WORKBOOK PAGES

'Tis pleasant, sure, to see one's name in print;
A Book's a Book, altho' there's nothing in't.

—Byron, *English Bards and Scotch Reviewers* (1809). II/ 51-2

Motivation (Chapter One)

Why would you like a collection of your poems published?

	✓
You want to leave a bit of yourself behind when you die	
You want them to find more readers.	
You want an heirloom for your children / grandchildren	
You want your memories preserved	
You want validation: proof your poems are worth all the effort you put into them	
You want to 'come out' as a poet	
You want something to sell at readings	
You're ambitious for your work: this is just the first step	
Because you write them, and the next stage must be to publish them	
Because your friends/family think you should	
To make money	
To draw attention to your work	
There's something you badly need to write about and only poetry will do	
There's someone you want to impress	
Because someone told you you'd never manage it	
You have a job as a creative writing tutor and you need more street-cred	
Your dad did it: you can do it	
Other reasons (write them in)	

Which publisher, and are you ready? (Chapter Three)

What have you done so far? How much do you know already? Where have you already had poems published? This doesn't have to be precisely accurate and it doesn't matter what your replies are.

Magazines (write in the names)	
Anthologies (titles)	
Newspapers	
Pamphlet (date and publisher)	
Book (date and publisher)	
Postcard	
Poster	
Website	
Ezine	
Other	

If you've already approached publishers, which ones and when?

If you've already entered any competitions for book or pamphlet collections, which ones, and when? Was there any feedback? e.g. short-listing, offer to put some of the poems into an anthology etc

Name the poetry editors of as many as you can:

Bloodaxe Books	
Red Squirrel	
Faber & Faber	
Carcanet	
Enitharmon	
Picador	
Cape	
CB editions	
Cinnamon	
Liverpool University Press (Pavilion Poetry)	
Seren	
Nine Arches	
Diehard Publishing	
Indigo Dreams	
Oversteps Books	
Worple Press	
Valley Press	
The Emma Press	
Freight Books	
Penned in the Margins	
Eyewear Publishing	

Name five poetry pamphlet imprints and their editors

Ten single collections of poetry you've read in the last two years: title, author and publisher

1.	
2.	
3.	
4.	
5.	
6.	
7.	
8.	
9.	
10.	

Making the web work for you (Chapter five)

Choose three publishers you would like to approach (see also following pages)

Name of publisher	Reasons for choice	What you're going to *tell* them to explain your choice
1.		
2.		
3.		

Poetry editor's name?	
Is the editor also a poet or a reviewer? What? Where? Have you read any?	
How long has the editor been in the game? Age? Background?	
How does submission work with this editor?	
Any books from this press shortlisted for prizes? If so, what?	
How many poetry books do they publish each year?	
How many first collections a year usually?	
Type of poetry they publish?	
Are any recent books from this publisher reviewed online? Anything useful in reviews?	
Typical track record of their poets	
How are they funded?	
What's the production quality of the books like?	
Any online interviews with editor?	
How do they promote / sell books?	
Names of poets you know published by this publisher	
House magazine?	

Poetry editor's name?	
Is the editor also a poet or a reviewer? What? Where? Have you read any?	
How long has the editor been in the game? Age? Background?	
How does submission work with this editor?	
Any books from this press shortlisted for prizes? If so, what?	
How many poetry books do they publish each year?	
How many first collections a year usually?	
Type of poetry they publish?	
Are any recent books from this publisher reviewed online? Anything useful in reviews?	
Typical track record of their poets	
How are they funded?	
What's the production quality of the books like?	
Any online interviews with editor?	
How do they promote / sell books?	
Names of poets you know published by this publisher	
House magazine?	

Poetry editor's name?	
Is the editor also a poet or a reviewer? What? Where? Have you read any?	
How long has the editor been in the game? Age? Background?	
How does submission work with this editor?	
Any books from this press shortlisted for prizes? If so, what?	
How many poetry books do they publish each year?	
How many first collections a year usually?	
Type of poetry they publish?	
Are any recent books from this publisher reviewed online? Anything useful in reviews?	
Typical track record of their poets	
How are they funded?	
What's the production quality of the books like?	
Any online interviews with editor?	
How do they promote / sell books?	
Names of poets you know published by this publisher	
House magazine?	

Publisher analysis / rating sheet

IMPRINT NAME:					
Outcomes: score 0 = low, 3 = high	**0-3**	**0-3**	**0-3**	**0-3**	**0-3**
Kudos					
Nice list / pleased to be on it					
Stability of imprint/ has it got a future?					
Process: score 0 = low, 3 = high	**0-3**	**0-3**	**0-3**	**0-3**	**0-3**
Good editor & editing style					
Editor I'd get on with					
Good fit with my own work					
Marketing / PR, sales, distribution etc					
Design:					
Values (& establishment or not)					
Total score:					

Plan A: End goal _____

	To be achieved this year
Year 1	
Year 2	
Year 3	
Year 4	
Year 5	

Plan B: End goal   _____

	To be achieved this year
Year 1	
Year 2	
Year 3	
Year 4	
Year 5	

More what ifs

e.g what if my book is nothing like *anything* in *anybody's* list?

Thinking outside the book

Less conventional options worth considering:

Notes on useful web resources

Blogs & info e.g. Tim Love's Literary References, Kim Moore's blog, Rogue Strands, Baroque in Hackney, The Bell Jar (Jo Bell's blog).Anthony Wilson's blog, Fiona Moore's *Displacement*, Charles Boyle's *SonofaBook*, desktopsallye, Poor Rude Lines, and add *at least* a dozen more below.

Poetry magazines to subscribe to or borrow

Ezines to follow and send poems to

Notes for poems

Notes for poems

Notes for poems